LAUNCH

PRAISE FOR LAUNCH

"Required reading for every teacher who cares. A dramatic re-framing and a road map on how to rebuild our schools from the inside."

–Seth Godin, author of *Stop Stealing Dreams*

"Educators and administrators are realizing that twenty-first-century education systems must change to focus on students being creators, innovators, and producers rather than passive receivers and consumers of often outdated information. It is driven by the belief and mindset that all students (and their teachers) can be creative; that everyone can be makers. John Spencer and A.J. Juliani have written an accessible and practical guide on how educators can integrate design thinking and making into their classroom teaching strategies. The *LAUNCH* framework that they present has the potential to dramatically change classrooms to be more engaging, student centric, and most of all, *fun!*"

–Dr. Jackie Gerstein, online faculty for master's degree programs in educational technology

"Spencer and Juliani are simultaneously bold and practical. They challenge the status quo of traditional classroom thinking while also holding the reader's hand through the day-to-day educational application of design thinking techniques. If you're ready to tap into the inherent creativity of all children (and teachers) and apply new lenses to learning and teaching, you'll learn a lot from this book."

–Scott McLeod, J.D., Ph.D., director of learning, teaching, and innovation, Prairie Lakes Area Education Agency

"*LAUNCH* will ignite the creative catalyst in every teacher who picks it up. *LAUNCH* is a digestible resource on the practice of designing thinking and how it can inspire the inherent maker in students. The result: teachers who design learning environments that inspire the humanity in all our students to think and act with compassion and creativity."

–David H. Clifford, senior learning experience designer, d.school K12 Lab, Hasso Plattner Institute of Design, Stanford Chief Catalyst and Founder, design school x

"For educators who value classrooms in which student choice and ownership of learning are non-negotiables, *LAUNCH* serves as a mentor resource for implementing these methods through design thinking and student-friendly motivational practices. A.J. and John thoughtfully wrote this book to empower creative, risk-taking teachers around the world who want to inspire innovation and think outside of traditional classroom practices."

–Kayla Delzer, elementary educator, TEDx speaker, innovation consultant

"Learn how to launch your own creative projects. John Spencer and A.J. Juliani have written a book that might not just launch learning in your classroom, but might just launch you to create the classroom of your dreams. Learning matters. You need the creativity to make it happen. Here's that book."

–**Vicki Davis**, @coolcatteacher, *Cool Cat Teacher Blog*, author of *Reinventing Writing*, host of *Every Classroom Matters*

"*LAUNCH* is a much-needed book to bring classrooms to life! The authors provide practical ideas, resources, and tips for teachers who want their learners to be creative, engaged, and innovative. Any teacher, even those who do not feel they are creative, will be inspired by the authors' personal stories and examples."

–**Shelly Sanchez Terrell**, teacher trainer and author of *The 30 Goals Challenge for Teachers and Learning to Go*

"If you are looking for a book with practical advice on how to embrace, empower, and unleash student creativity and innovation, *LAUNCH* is that book. Spencer and Juliani have created a clear roadmap to 'launch' your classroom with practical examples grounded in sound educational pedagogy."

–**Josh Stumpenhorst**, Illinois Teacher of the Year, author of *The New Teacher Revolution*

"In this increasingly connected world, educators may find themselves drowning in a sea of buzzwords. While we know that innovation and creativity are optimal, sometimes it's difficult to find an entry point to integrate best practices into our classrooms. This text, crafted by John and A.J., provides educators with a series of actionable steps regarding design thinking, while simultaneously dispelling common myths and dissolving perceived roadblocks to success."

–**Sarah Thomas**, founder EduMatch

"A brilliant and much-needed solution to a real problem. A fun and inspiring read, *LAUNCH* is a great way to organize curriculum, with useful lesson plan suggestions, too."

–**Derek Sivers**, founder of CD Baby, author of *Anything You Want*

"The future GIP (global innovation products) depend on more and more people developing and sharing their creative confidence and capacity to make. In their new book, Spencer and Juliani graciously share a fabulous dimension of their collaborative innovation engine for enhancing GIP–and bettering education. For me, their work strikes a powerful synthesis, combining the inspirational and the practical. With the chapters and various tools provided in *LAUNCH*, people in schools and other learning organizations will feel encouraged to build their own creative abilities and share the tender and fuel of growth mindset with others. Educators and facilitators will feel empowered to act and experiment because of the great scaffolding and materials the authors share."

–**Bo Adams**, chief innovation officer MViFi

"We all want our students to be more creative, to unlock their inner potential, and to work collaboratively in dynamic teams to do so. The problem is, we all struggle to know how. In *LAUNCH*, Spencer and Juliani use engaging prose and easy-to-follow outlines to take us from our utopian daydreams into a reality where students actually share their creations with the world. Every creative teacher I know has been waiting for a resource like this to help move their learners from the conceptual to the concrete."

–Royan Lee, teacher and blogger

"*LAUNCH* is an incredibly engaging book that helps teachers and students design creative learning experiences in classrooms and creates the imperative for rethinking the ways we educate our children in general. Change your classroom, change your school, and maybe even change the world!"

–Will Richardson, author of *Why School*, founder of Modernlearners.com

"*LAUNCH: Using Design Thinking to Boost Creativity and Bring Out the Maker in Every Student* provides a framework that is poised to spark a creative movement in schools across the world! It is a practical and valuable resource that is sure to unleash the creative power in all of our learners!"

–Laura Fleming, author of *Worlds of Making*

"In their book, *LAUNCH: Using Design Thinking to Boost Creativity and Bring Out the Maker in Every Student,* John Spencer and A.J. Juliani have taken their powerful ideas and expertise as long-time educators and boiled down practical advice that is inspiring as well as meaningful. This book is a true must-read for educators and administrators; it is chicken soup for the mind and provides frameworks on how to make a powerful shift to enhance the creative power of learning in the classroom."

–Adam Bellow, White House Innovation Fellow

"'Creativity' and 'innovation' are not words that are reserved for the few, but are opportunities that are available to everyone. Spencer and Juliani do an amazing job of bringing this concept to life using both powerful and practical examples, as well as narratives that make this book both inspiring and attainable at the same time. All kids walk into school curious and creative. This book will help weave a path to ensure that these traits are not only maintained, but accentuated when those same students leave."

–George Couros, author of *The Innovator's Mindset*

"*LAUNCH* is a powerful book for any teacher who wants to transform their classroom into a space where students' creativity and passion are valued. This is a book of practical pathways to unlock the big ideas of design thinking and project-based learning so that kids can make, do, reflect, and think in ways that can be transformative to the way our students think about school."

–Chris Lehmann, founding principal, Science Leadership Academy and co-author of *Building School 2.0: How to Create the Schools We Need*

"*LAUNCH* will propel all educators to think differently about how we bring creativity and innovation into our classrooms and schools. Critical thinking and problem solving are two important skills that all children must learn. After reading this book, you will have a renewed passion for helping to build an entire generation of creative thinkers."

–Salome Thomas-EL, award-winning principal and author

"Often times, teachers and administrators are left with overly abstract and complex resources regarding how to make the instructional shift to inquiry-based learning. *LAUNCH* is the exception as it cuts through the clutter, demystifies what design thinking is all about, and leaves readers inspired and proclaiming, 'I can do this!' This book is for all educators who are looking to infuse classrooms with more innovation and creativity."

–Ross Cooper, supervisor of instructional practice K-12,
Apple Distinguished Educator

"In *LAUNCH*, John Spencer and A.J. Juliani take readers on a journey to a land of creative possibility. By offering their own put-it-out-there-and-see-what-happens twist on design thinking, Spencer and Juliani both channel the spirit of Seymour Pappert and help us understand how any classroom can be transformed into a place of invention and innovation–a place where ideas take flight."

–Edward Clapp, Ed.D, project director at Project Zero,
author of *Participatory Creativity*

"Never before have I seen design thinking packaged quite as beautifully as A.J. Juliani and John Spencer have done in *LAUNCH*. This book should be every teacher's road map for bringing design thinking to life in his or her classroom, from start to finish. This fresh, smart way of helping everyone to understand and embrace the design-thinking process will be talked about for years to come. Bravo, Juliani and Spencer!"

–Amy Mascott, creator of teachmama.com and
co-author of *Raising a Rock-Star Reader*

LAUNCH

Using Design Thinking to
Boost Creativity and Bring Out
the Maker in Every Student

John Spencer and A.J. Juliani

Illustrated by John Spencer

LAUNCH:
Using Design Thinking to Boost Creativity and Bring Out the Maker in Every Student
© 2016 by John Spencer and A.J. Juliani

This book is available at special discounts when purchased in quantity for use as premiums, promotions, fundraisers, or for educational use. For inquiries and details, contact the publisher at shelley@daveburgessconsulting.com.

Published by Dave Burgess Consulting, Inc.
San Diego, CA
http://daveburgessconsulting.com

Cover Design by Genesis Kohler
Editing and Interior Design by My Writers' Connection

Library of Congress Control Number: 2016939840
Paperback ISBN: 978-0-9969895-4-1
Ebook ISBN: 978-0-9969895-5-8

First Printing: May 2016

DEDICATION

We dedicate this book ...

... to every teacher who is taking creative risks in their classroom,

... to every teacher who is guiding students on a creative journey and supporting innovative work in their school,

... and to every teacher who is breaking out of the status quo and empowering a future generation of makers.

It is dedicated to Mr. Flynn, my (A.J.) high school math teacher who told me to take a computer programming class (even after I almost failed pre-calculus). It's dedicated to Mrs. Haring who handpicked books for me to read and stretched my imagination further than I realized.

It is dedicated to Mrs. Smoot and Mr. Darrow, my (John) middle-school History Day advisors, who saw something creative in me and found a way for me to make something meaningful and who changed my life forever as a result.

As teachers using design thinking, we stand on the shoulders of giants. People like David and Tom Kelley, Tim Brown, Roger Martin, Jeanne Liedtka, John Maeda, Susie Wise, Peter Rowe, and so many others who have brought design thinking into business, education, and our world. They've shaped our lives with their work, and our book is shaped by their many contributions to design thinking and the creative process.

Contents

WE BELIEVE...

We believe that all kids are naturally creative and that every classroom should be filled with creativity and wonder.

We want to see teachers unleash the creative potential in all of their students so that kids can be makers, designers, artists, and engineers.

We know that school can be busy. Materials can be scarce. The creative process can seem confusing, especially when you have a tight curriculum map. So creativity becomes a side project, an enrichment activity you get to when you have time for it. But the thing is, there's never enough time.

We can do better.

We believe that creative thinking is as vital as math or reading or writing. There's power in problem-solving and experimenting and taking things from questions to ideas to authentic products that you launch to the world. Something happens in students when they define themselves as makers and inventors and creators.

That's the power of design thinking. It provides a flexible framework for creative work. It's used in engineering, publishing, business, the humanities, in non-profit and community work. And yes, it can be used in education! You can use it in every subject with every age group. Although there are many versions of design thinking, we have developed the LAUNCH Cycle as a student-friendly way to engage in design thinking.

We believe all students deserve the opportunity to be their best creative selves, both in and out of school. We believe all kids are unique, authentic, and destined to be original.

Most importantly, we believe this is not an all-encompassing solution, but a start. We believe our role is to empower kids to make an impact on the world around them and fully believe in themselves.

It is because of these beliefs that we wrote this book. We wrote it for ourselves, for our colleagues, for our friends, for our students, and for you. Because ultimately, we believe that you have the power to inspire kids and create a ripple effect that lasts for years to come.

CHAPTER 1
WE NEED CREATIVE CLASSROOMS

Never believe that a few caring people
can't change the world.
For, indeed, that's all who ever have.

– Margaret Mead

You've seen them. The most successful people in the world aren't defeated by change; they thrive on it. They build solutions and problem-solve on the fly. They make products that serve thousands, even millions, of people. They are creative.

And their creativity helps them navigate new technology, new problems, and new environments. Their creativity gives them the tool set to succeed in a world where there is no proven path and no guarantee that anything will stay the same.

This is why so many people have pushed for more creative classrooms. It's why videos about creativity in education go viral. It's why the Maker Movement has filled schools around the world, inspiring young minds to build, tinker, and play.

Yet, as a classroom teacher or school leader, you know that after years of honing standardized, formulaic processes, making the shift to innovative teaching and learning is not as easy as snapping your fingers and saying, "*Voilà!* Let's put creativity back into our schools!"

THE NEW DIGITAL DIVIDE IS LESS ABOUT ACCESS AND ALL ABOUT CREATIVE OPPORTUNITIES.

When we talk with teachers around the world about creativity, here's what we hear:

- "Yes, I want my students to be creative, but I don't have enough materials. Do you know how much that technology and maker equipment cost? My school doesn't have the funds for that!"

- "How are we supposed to be doing creative work when following a scripted curriculum? It seems impossible to cover all the standards and prepare my students for these assessments, let alone give them *time* to create and make."

- "I see all of these examples of creative work students are doing on Twitter, blogs, and education conferences, but I don't know how to actually pull that off in my classroom. I've never been trained on these methods, and it seems hard to make it all work smoothly."

- "I've done creative projects and innovative learning in my classroom before, and I've gotten into trouble for it. I've had parents saying I'm not teaching. I've had principals say my classroom was a mess. I don't have the support and permission from my school to do this type of creative work."

- "I know that my students should be doing project-based learning, making, and creating, but I'm just not a creative person. I'm a good teacher, but I don't think I can keep coming up with all kinds of creative ideas for my students."

- "My students are too young to be designing things. We should really just focus on the fundamentals."

- "Creativity is important, but I don't know if that would work in my subject area."

We want to say it loud and clear: We hear you! These issues are real. Change is often difficult, confusing, and even painful. But we also know that our world is changing. With the proliferation of digital devices, we now have the ability to connect to the world anywhere at any time. We now carry around powerful devices that allow us to create content that had previously been costly and cumbersome.

In the past, we heard about the "digital divide" between those who had access to technology and those who didn't. We are now seeing a new divide emerge—a Creative Chasm between those who passively consume and those who actively create. We see it with the students who spend hours watching videos on their phones, while a few bold students create their own YouTube channels where they film, edit, and launch to an authentic audience. We see it with students who download games, while a few students design their own video games.

Our current model of schooling amplifies this Creative Chasm. From the bell schedule to the grading system to the lesson planning and pedagogy, our students inhabit factory-styled schools. Phrases like "content delivery" and "delivering a lesson" treat education as a commodity to be collected and then used in the future. This model might have worked in developing compliant factory workers. So here we are now, well into the twenty-first century. The factories are gone. The jobs have moved overseas. Yet, this industrial school model remains.

Here's what happens: students grow up immersed in a consumer culture and then attend schools where they consume rather than create knowledge. The chasm widens and students graduate without the creative capacity to navigate the ever-changing landscape of a globalized economy. On a more personal level, they miss out on the deeply human joy of designing and making.

How do we bridge this divide? How do we create innovative spaces where all students can thrive? How do we transform classrooms into bastions of creativity and wonder? And how do we do this when we have limited resources, scarce time, and the constant bombardment of high-stakes testing? These challenges are real, but they aren't insurmountable. We have both experienced these challenges ourselves as public school educators.

But we've also learned something along the way: behind each of these challenges is an opportunity to innovate.

What about the Test?

We live in an era where test scores are mistaken for learning. Teachers are afraid of low scores. They're afraid of being judged. Innovation is risky in a culture that values compliance over creativity.

We realize that the risk is real. We have experienced this ourselves. However, we also know that design thinking isn't about abandoning the standards. It's about raising the standards and challenging students to think at a deeper level. In our experience, when students are thinking creatively, they are fully engaged in their learning. This increased student engagement often leads to more buy-in from students and ultimately deeper learning. Although they still hate the tests, they often view testing as something easy and annoying, because they have already experienced authentic challenges that pushed their thinking to go beyond filling in bubbles.

There is no guarantee that creative thinking will increase test scores, but who would you rather have take a test: a disengaged trained test-taker or a fully engaged creative thinker?

What If There's Not Enough Time?

You might have a rigid, fast-paced curriculum map. While you would love to do creative projects, you find yourself tossing these into the spare moments you have. So you do a culminating project or a special day before a holiday break. In the process, creativity is a side dish or maybe even dessert, while the "real content" is your main dish. But what if creativity isn't a dish at all? What if creativity is a totally different way of cooking? What if creativity means you abandon pre-packaged meals and empower your students to be the chefs?

In this book, we'll explore design thinking as a framework for learning. It isn't a separate subject that you need to squeeze into an already busy schedule. Instead, it's a different way of doing things that will actually free up your time.

SOMETIMES THE BEST "TECHNOLOGY" IS A ROLL OF DUCT TAPE.

What If I Don't Have Enough Resources?

You don't need a makerspace or a 3-D printer to do creative projects in your classroom. You don't need the latest gadgets or the most cutting-edge apps. Some of our favorite materials have been duct tape and cardboard or a notebook and pencils. We love technology, but the greatest creative asset you have is the human mind.

We noticed this recently when we launched the Global Day of Design. We developed this as a way for teachers to try out the LAUNCH Cycle in a single day. To our surprise, teachers who had never used design thinking began using the resources months before the official Global Day of Design. Their classrooms became hubs of innovation. These teachers were leading creative movements within their districts.

And yet few of these classrooms were "techie" in the traditional sense. They weren't one-to-one. They didn't have 3-D printers. However, they were launching their students in creative projects using whatever resources they had, and the results went far beyond their expectations.

What If I Fail?

You will fail. It's going to happen. You will have moments when your students get frustrated with the design process. You will have class periods that tank. However, failure is a part of the process for innovative teachers. Each mistake is simply another iteration on the journey toward success.

See, you are a trail blazer and the only way you blaze a trail is by taking risks and failing forward. With design thinking, you have the tools and you have a map. But you are navigating tricky terrain. You are going where the roads aren't paved and danger lurks at every corner. However, it's an epic adventure. Your students will be forever changed.

EVERY MISTAKE IS
SIMPLY ANOTHER ITERATION
CLOSER TO SUCCESS.

What If I'm Not Very Creative?

When you consider the word "creative," you might think of a painter, a playwright, an author, a photographer, a filmmaker, or a chef. In other words, you might think of people who make things. I think it's what we mean when we use a label like "creative type."

But there is no such thing as a creative type. We are all creative. Every one of us. We just need a bigger definition of creativity.

Yes, creativity involves making things. But it can also mean mashing up ideas in innovative ways. It can mean geeking out on data and finding unique solutions to practical problems. It can mean hacking systems and tweaking things in unusual ways. It can mean exploring ideas and navigating information until you become an expert curator. It can mean designing systems that empower the creative work of others. It can mean creating change in the world by speaking truth and leading movements and interacting with people. See, each of these creative approaches shapes our world in profound ways.

And the more we see the creativity all around us, the more we are able to appreciate the creativity inside ourselves. As a teacher, this means you can work out of your own creative strengths while tapping into the creative potential of your students. In other words, you don't have to be a "creative type" to have a creative classroom.

CREATIVITY IS FOR ALL OF US.

THE SURPRISING TRUTH ABOUT CREATIVITY

The problem is that almost everything you've heard about creativity in our schools is wrong. These myths about creativity that pop up in business books, TED talks, and the evening news all make it seem like something unattainable—unless you have a big breakthrough idea and are letting your students be free to create at all times.

It's time we stop listening to the myth that creative work is for the select, gifted few. Let's work together to break down the barriers that keep us—and our students—from unleashing our creative minds.

Creativity is for all of us. And in this book, we'll show you how to boost creativity and spark innovation in yourself, your school, in any classroom, and with every student.

As classroom teachers, we each spent hours and hours trying to unlock the creativity inside our students. Through project-based learning, inquiry-based learning, genius hour, independent projects, authentic learning experiences, and challenge-based learning opportunities, we saw firsthand what worked—and what failed.

If you are frustrated by the barriers and obstacles in your way right now, don't try to put them to the side. Don't try to hide them. Embrace the frustration and use it to motivate your creative spirit and innovative approach to teaching and learning.

Creativity Is a Process That Requires Structure

The word *structure* gets a bad rap as being part of some sort of rigid process that takes away from authentic and creative learning. That's simply not the case. Structure provides the outline for a song, the dimensions for an architectural wonder, and the steps for a successful launch into space!

Forget what you have been told about creativity and innovation. Forget the notion that structure limits this type of work. Forget the idea of the lone creative genius with complete freedom changing the world. In the coming chapters, we'll introduce you to a specific process and practical framework that will immediately impact the creativity in your classroom.

Design Thinking Is the Process

Design thinking provides a way to think about creative work. It starts with empathy, working to really understand the problems people are facing before attempting to create solutions.

The LAUNCH Cycle Is the Framework

The LAUNCH Cycle is not a formula. It is not a step-by-step guide to being creative. However, we've used the LAUNCH Cycle framework to make creativity an authentic experience time and time again in our classrooms.

The LAUNCH Cycle outlines creative work from start to finish. From listening and learning, to navigating ideas, to highlighting what works, the LAUNCH Cycle builds capacity and clarity for teachers and students who are making, building, tinkering, and creating. The final piece of the LAUNCH Cycle is what sets it apart: actually launching your creation out into the world!

IT'S TIME TO THINK INSIDE THE BOX

The students gather around nervously before the movie. The place is packed and buzzing with anticipation. The filmmakers can't wait to see their movie on the big screen at this Grand Rapids movie theater. But it's not a Hollywood Blockbuster, and the men and women walking down the red carpet aren't the elite actors and actresses you might expect. Instead, the guests of honor are World War II heroes, and the filmmakers are high school students from Kent Innovation High School.

The students have spent months on this project, but the journey was worth it. As the stories unfold on screen, the students look around and see the crowd laughing and crying—success! The night is an unforgettable experience that they will treasure for a lifetime.

People typically think of creativity and innovation as something that happens "outside the box." But the research and people we profile in this book, like the students from Kent Innovation High School, would disagree. The most creative and innovative work comes from circumstances that force a new type of thinking for solutions *inside* the box. If you're skeptical that creativity can thrive despite limitations, consider this: The World War II documentary project was a huge success. And as you'll read in a moment, that success wasn't confined to a single night. These students didn't have fancy gadgets or 3-D printers; they shot their videos with cell phones. And just like your students, the kids at Kent Innovation High School had to take standardized tests.

The teachers at Kent Innovation understood that their greatest assets weren't shiny new pieces of equipment or a slick set of software. It was the creative genius of their students. It was the power of design thinking that unleashed the creative potential in every student. It was the power of a *launch*—of telling a real story to a real audience and thus empowering the students to see themselves as storytellers, creators, makers, and historians.

THE MISSING PIECE TO THE CREATIVE PROCESS: LAUNCHING

A year after the screening, I (John) visited with student filmmakers and talked with them about the project. One student mentioned that the daughter of one of the soldiers had contacted him. The former soldier had passed away, and the family wanted to share part of his story at the memorial service.

"She said that he had never shared his story with the family, and she wanted to thank me for telling it," the student said. He paused for a second and then continued, "It hit me that this is why we made this film. If we hadn't, the stories would have disappeared forever."

Isn't that kind of meaning and purpose what we want for our students? Don't we want total student engagement? Don't we want students to be empowered to own the learning process? Don't we want students to view themselves as makers and creators?

Sure we do. But what do we do with all the things that keep us from innovating? What do we do, for example, with the self-doubt that stifles our creative ideas?

SEE CREATIVITY FOR WHAT IT IS

When you see creativity as something to find or acquire, it becomes an act of hoping and wishing for a great idea or moment. In contrast, when you understand that creativity is something you can unleash and bring out of yourself, it becomes an internal act of opening up and using those creative muscles that every one of us possesses.

Creative teachers aren't *only* the teachers whose students work in makerspaces, build apps and websites, do artwork, and act in productions.

Creative students aren't *only* the students who have high IQ scores, tend to be extroverts, and spend time making projects on their own.

Creative teachers are coaches, club sponsors, and classroom leaders who challenge their students daily to think deeply, argue critically, and solve problems. Creative students may be quiet, can often work better as a team member, and tend to respond to intrinsic challenges. Remove the bias about who is creative and who is not creative. You might just surprise yourself.

Making without launching is like cooking a four-course meal and eating it alone. It may taste phenomenal, but you'll be the only one who knows. How sad for others to miss out on the flavor explosion! And how unfortunate that you'd have no validation from anyone else on the planet as to whether the meal tastes as good to another person.

Yet this is what we do time and time again in our schools. We consistently ask our students to make art for themselves, put on play productions for their class, and write poems that only the teacher will read.

What if instead of taking that piece of artwork created in second grade home to Mom and Dad to put on the fridge, we took our students to a nursing home and had them share their art with our elders? What if instead of putting our students' haiku on the bulletin board outside of our room, we compiled them into a Kindle book and launched it on Amazon? What if instead of having our students present a book report in front of the class, we live-streamed it on YouTube and shared it with the author's fans?

When we go through the creative process and stop it after students make something, we are missing out on the biggest opportunity for authentic learning to happen. Launching our work into the real world and in front of an actual audience is what makes creative work so scary, but also so rewarding.

We wrote this book to help you unlock the creativity in your classroom and take it to the next level. We want to make it real, refreshing, and empowering to all of your students—and you, as well! And guess what? We want to show you the exact process, framework, and structure that we've used with students of all ages to unleash creativity. The process and framework we uncover has catapulted businesses, organizations, and entrepreneurs into success because it works in so many different situations with so many types of people and products.

As you continue reading, you'll find that creativity is very inspiring but also very practical. You'll find that innovative work is less spontaneous and more process driven. You'll find that frameworks and limitations help the creative process rather than hindering its potential. Most of all, you'll find that creative work is fun and doable in any type of classroom.

THE SILVER LINING: INNOVATION OUT OF FRUSTRATION

A few years ago, I (A.J.) was frustrated by the fact that the only thing my eleventh grade students cared about in my class was their grade. Because of this frustration, I decided to launch a 20% project[1]. Taking a cue from Google, I allotted 20 percent of our class time to exploration. I told students to follow their interests and curiosity, research a specific topic, create a product out of that research, and share it with the world in TED-talk-style live-streamed presentations. Students were more motivated than I'd ever seen in all my years of teaching because it was coming from a place inside themselves, not from an extrinsic reward. They learned sign language, made computers, rebuilt car engines, and learned how to play the guitar. One student even tried to clone a carnivorous plant! The project was successful because it empowered students to learn and create based on their interests and passions, not our (adult) needs and curriculum.

Like frustration, desperation can be the trigger for innovation. Human rights violations and genocide are tough topics. Having students read articles and watch a few videos wasn't cutting it. Invariably, after discussing these heart-wrenching issues, students always feel the need to "do something" to help. Out of my desperation to find a better way to teach this unit, my students and I established a collaborative project called *Project: Global Inform*.

The original idea was to send letters and e-mails to senators about human rights violations, but my students took that idea and turned it into something far better. They partnered with other students in their school who were passionate about the same issues to create an awareness campaign. Using multi-media presentations and social media, they worked to inform their classmates, school, community, and larger global audience about these difficult issues.

Innovation can benefit *any* area of education. For example, staff members at Wissahickon school district felt frustrated about having to spend an in-service day learning about a tool they were already using. Their very appropriate question was, *Why have the same training when everyone is on different levels?* We developed our *game-based professional development missions* in answer to that frustration.

A fantastic teacher with whom I work with was frustrated that "Industrial Arts" (shop class) still looked, for the most part, like it did when he was in high school. After a lot of hard work, he turned that frustration into a new ninth-grade course, Creative Design and Engineering, and a reworking of the entire scope and sequence to create a true Maker Department at our high school.

The lesson? If we allow frustration to get the better of us, we miss the silver lining: Innovative ideas can often come out of working through frustration to a creative end.

WHICH PATH WILL YOU CHOOSE?

You've seen it before. Someone launches a program or an app that promises to revolutionize education. "This is the future of learning!" a pundit will proclaim. Suddenly, articles pop up promising that this new product will replace teachers and change education forever.

We know better. The future of education can't be found in a gadget or app or program or product. It doesn't require a think-tank full of pundits. No, the future of education can be found in your classroom. Your classroom is packed with creative potential. You have all the innovation you need right there in your room. You have the power to make it happen.

It's what happens when you experiment. It's what happens when you give your students voice and choice. It's what happens when you abandon the scripted curriculum and take your students off-road in their learning. It's what happens when you teach to your students rather than teaching to the test. It's what happens when you unleash the creative power of all of your students, when you make the bold decision to let them make things, design things, and solve problems that they find relevant.

THE FUTURE OF EDUCATION IS ALREADY INSIDE YOUR CLASSROOM.

Sometimes it's messy and even confusing. It often looks humble. But understand this: Every time your students get the chance to be authors, filmmakers, scientists, artists, and engineers, you are planting the seeds for a future you could have never imagined on your own. And that right there is the beauty of creative classrooms. That's the power of innovative teachers. And the truth is, that is why the future of education is *you*. You are the hero of your classroom's story. You are the one who can transform the learning so that all of your students can reach their creative potential.

Design thinking isn't the answer. *You* are the answer. You are the one who can make it happen. The LAUNCH Cycle is a powerful set of tools that you can use as you build the type of learning spaces your students need. But the solution is still you. We are sharing some great tools, but ultimately, the tools are still in your hands.

Too many educators believe they have lost their creativity—or that they were never creative in the first place. Maybe they stopped creating because they didn't think they had the time, energy, or mental capacity for new ideas. We don't buy it. Not creating is a choice—and a poor choice at that. And in truth, every time you come up with a new idea for a lesson, you *are* creating. Every time you think of a way to handle that super-challenging student, you are creating. Every time you collaborate with a colleague, design your classroom, set up the desks in a new way, or do something different—you are creating! What would it mean to take that creativity to the next level?

This book gives you a framework to see creativity and innovation in the classroom through a new lens. This lens empowers you as the teacher and leader to build creative capacity, set structures that increase opportunities for innovation, and set your students up to launch their work to an authentic audience.

The choice is yours. Come alongside us, join the creative revolution, and LAUNCH into learning!

Visit TheLaunchCycle.com to get more information and resources as you read the book. Join the discussion online using the hashtag #launchbook.

Notes

1. http://ajjuliani.com/20-time-guide

CHAPTER 2
FINDING YOUR CREATIVE APPROACH

We rarely create something different until we experience something different.

- George Couros
in *The Innovator's Mindset*

In March 1970, the United States sent three astronauts on a mission to the moon. Apollo 13 was a follow-up flight to successful moon landings of Apollo 11 and 12. But when this rocket launched into orbit, no one realized the ingenuity and creativity that would be needed to bring the astronauts back home safely.

After an explosion of an oxygen tank in the spacecraft's service module, NASA's Mission Control cancelled Apollo 13's moon landing and told the astronauts to move into the lunar module. The smaller space demanded less fuel to operate, which allowed the crew to reserve their limited power for re-entry.

Soon after the move, NASA engineers realized they had a major problem: the carbon dioxide levels in the lunar module were climbing. It had been built to carry two astronauts for thirty-six hours, yet it would take the three astronauts ninety-six hours to get home.

Ed Smylie was sitting at home watching the mission on TV when he heard the now famous words, "Houston, we have a problem."

Smylie, who oversaw NASA's Crew Systems Division, rushed to the space center to meet with his unheralded band of engineers. Their task: fit a square peg into a round hole, *before* the crew members ran out of oxygen.

The Crew Systems Division, comprised of engineers and scientists of all backgrounds, had to find a way to replace the lunar module's carbon dioxide scrubbers. The problem was that the lunar module had circular scrubbers and the only spare carbon dioxide scrubbers aboard were the square ones from the space craft's command module.

The Crew Systems Division worked at a breakneck pace to put together an improvised adapter using all sorts of random parts, like a flight manual cover, suit parts, and socks. The team used the CAPCOM (Capsule Communicator) to transmit the assembly instructions to the astronauts who were already starting to feel the effects of the poisonous gas even as they put together what they called the "mailbox rig."

And then, while everyone back home watched, it worked.

This story was brought to life in the film *Apollo 13*, and if you've seen the movie, you'll remember the loud cheer that echoed through the space center when the levels of carbon dioxide began dropping and oxygen filled the module for the astronauts' trip home.

In those intense, pressure-filled moments, the Crew Systems Division was challenged to think about and create a solution using finite resources in a limited amount of time.

Sound familiar?

The myth is that creativity is the outcome of complete freedom. The reality is quite the opposite. Creativity often stems from pain and conflict. It starts with problems we encounter and situations where time, resources, and information are limited.

What the film didn't show viewers were the massive hours of preparation and training everyone at NASA underwent before taking part in the mission. They spent days working on unimaginable situations and coming up with creative solutions. Astronauts have to be physically fit, mentally sharp, and Mac-Gyver-like in their ability to assess a situation and develop a rapid response.

And the astronauts come from all walks of life. They are engineers, scientists, athletes, doctors, professors, programmers, and designers. Each of their unique backgrounds plays an integral role in solving a problem like the one faced by the Crew Systems Division during the Apollo 13 mission.

Teaching is no different. Except we don't get to go to space.

Teachers come from all walks of life. We bring with us a variety of skills and life experiences from unique backgrounds. We majored in different areas at college, took up various interests in school, and work on different projects and hobbies as adults. We each have a distinct personality, skill set, and story.

And we are *all* creative. We each have to solve problems quickly, come up with collaborative solutions, and manage multiple personalities and issues on a daily basis. Rather than labeling some teachers as creative and others as not-so-creative, we hold the bold belief that all teachers possess the potential for creativity. We also believe that schools benefit when every teacher taps into their own creative approach.

We Are All Creative

I (John) stood in front of our brightly colored mural, admiring the blending on the sunset that Juan had created, and marveling at the minute details Maria had painted.

A math teacher stopped and stared.

"It's impressive," she said.

"Thanks," I answered. "The kids worked hard on this."

She nodded. "I'm glad you can give them a creative outlet. I'm not much of a creative type, but I think it's cool when teachers lead projects like this."

Creative type. That term has been tossed my way since my first year of teaching. I develop my lessons from scratch. I integrate art into the curriculum. I sketch ridiculous cartoons on my board. I enjoy building technology platforms and writing books in my spare time.

I'm that guy. The "creative type."

But here's the thing: so is every other teacher.

When that math teacher said, "I'm not much of a creative type," she failed to recognize the creativity inherent in problem-solving. My students painted murals, but she had students comparing and contrasting approaches to linear equations. Her students were working on a budget project that pushed divergent thinking in a way that was reminiscent of *Apollo 13*.

Schools often hold a narrow view of creativity, relegating it to the art room and maybe some fun crafts in class. Sometimes, "creative type" is used in a derogatory way. It's the teacher with the messy desk or the craft supplies scattered all over the room. Or it's the opposite. You know the type with the tidy spaces and the immaculate bulletin boards and the themes that actually look like the pictures from Pinterest. And if that's you, I promise I'm not mocking it. I'm truly jealous, because I tried to make a bulletin board pretty once, and the results were disastrous.

The truth is that there is no single creative type. There are many creative types who offer unique gifts—all of which can transform learning and spark innovation. The more we recognize the diversity of the creative mindset, the better we become at integrating creativity into the culture and curriculum of the classroom. In the process, we not only thrive in our creative identity but we honor our students' creativity.

What Is Your Creative Approach?

Apollo 13 could have easily turned into one of the most tragic space stories of all time had the heroic Crew Systems Division not solved a complex, real-world problem by working collaboratively. Each person brought a unique creative mindset to the specific design challenge. The fact that these individuals possessed different strengths, skills, information, and talent is what made the collective project successful. The same is true of our schools today. Before talking more about collaboration, it may be helpful to understand the individual—you—and how to unleash your unique creative ability.

The following are some of the creative approaches teachers can use in developing creative classrooms. As you read through each one, think about which type you connect with the most. Remember that none of these are inherently better than the others. They are simply a lens for how to view creative work.

BRAIN BOOST
THE EUREKA MOMENT MYTH OF CREATIVITY

Researcher Vera-John Steiner interviewed more than seventy living creative geniuses and analyzed the notebooks of fifty deceased thought-leaders (including Tolstoy, Einstein, etc.). In seeking to understand their work habits, she came across a common trait that completely dismissed the notion of a singular moment of creative inspiration:

> *"Creativity started with the notebooks' sketches and jottings, and only later resulted in a pure, powerful idea. The one characteristic that all of these creatives shared— whether they were painters, actors, or scientists— was how often they put their early thoughts and inklings out into the world, in sketches, dashed-off phrases and observations, bits of dialogue, and quick prototypes. Instead of arriving in one giant leap, great creations emerged by zigs and zags as their creators engaged over and over again with these externalized images."*

Where are you giving students chances to "zig and zag" in their learning?

Do you give yourself permission to tinker and create as a teacher and/or leader?

1. THE ARTIST

This teacher loves to create things from scratch. You'll see this teacher working all summer developing new materials and dreaming up new projects for students. Although the Artist will explore other resources, the purpose is typically inspiration rather than adoption. Some teachers might consider it a waste of time to design every lesson from scratch. Why reinvent the wheel? But to the Artist, a better question might be, *why not* reinvent the wheel? The world would be pretty boring if every wheel looked the same!

For the Artist, teaching is less about systems or structures and more about designing plans, activities, and classroom settings that kids will love. If anything, the Artist might rail against any structure that seems to stifle creative work. So when Artists scoff at a new initiative, it isn't meant to be negative. They are genuinely baffled by the fact that someone would create a roadblock in the journey toward creating something new, and they are sensitive to how soul-crushing standardized systems can be for kids engaged in creative work.

These teachers thrive in environments with creative autonomy. They tend to view creativity as natural, messy, and inherently, well, normal. For the Artists, discussions about data feel cold and sterile compared with the vibrant stories of learning.

2. THE GEEK

This teacher is creative in the sense of being fascinated by ideas and constantly working to tweak things. Systems and structures are as fascinating to the Geek as ideas and content. This teacher wants to make something new but also wants to explore existing models and monitor effectiveness with data (albeit data that is actually accurate and meaningful). Where the Artist views creativity as messy, the Geek sees value in creating order from chaos.

If you're anything like us, you cringe a little when you hear the words "research-based" or "data-driven." But for the Geek, these terms aren't inherently bad so much as misunderstood. The Geek loves all things informational. Theory isn't simply theory. It's a framework for making sense out of why things happen. Research isn't some far-off concept. It's what allows us to know what works. It's easy to miss the creativity here because it is often nuanced and complex. However, to the Geek, systems are like mental playgrounds that exist to be explored.

The Geek might not always look creative compared to the Artist because the new things he creates don't always have an overtly artistic flair. However, Geeks can remind schools that sometimes creativity happens *through* systems and structures. Sometimes creativity works best within a framework informed by the data we collect on a regular basis.

When a Geek works collaboratively with an Artist, the pairing is like a beautiful song and dance—one complements the other. And their example reminds us all that systems and stories are both inherently valuable and connected to our shared experiences as teachers.

3. THE ARCHITECT

Like the Geek, the Architect is able to see the systematic side of creativity. However, while the Geek focuses on making small iterations and tweaking the system, the Architect enjoys designing and developing new systems from scratch.

In many cases, the Architect isn't viewed as being a creative type because she relies on the collaborative work of other creative types to design something. In these situations, the Architect doesn't seem to be a "maker," because the systems she creates seem seamless and almost invisible. But like any true architecture, those invisible structures have a profound influence on people.

See, the best Architects are able to articulate a creative vision in a way that bridges the individual messiness of the Artist with the systems thinking of the Geek. The result is something that doesn't initially appear to be creative so much as "hands-off" leadership. However, the best Architects are masters at getting other creative types to work collaboratively by designing an invisible system where creativity thrives. And the Architect does this by thinking intentionally about systems and people, and about science and art.

4. THE ENGINEER

While the Architect designs new systems, the Engineer tends to focus on fixing problems. So the history text is dead-boring? How can we fix it? How can we add something new? What can we replace? What can we mix up? A sort of *Mythbusters* hypothesis-testing drives this creative approach; the Engineer is always on the search for a better solution.

Unlike the Artist, this teacher doesn't feel compelled to reinvent the wheel every time. If a great resource out there works, why bother making something new? To the Engineer, creativity is found in constantly trying, testing, analyzing, and refining. However, unlike the Geek, the Engineer is able to abandon frameworks and ignore data in order to think divergently about a problem. If the Geek wants to know *why* things work, the Engineer is more interested in *how* things work and in how to do things differently.

The creativity of an Engineer may not always be obvious because it looks so practical and hands-on. Like the math teacher mentioned before, these types of teachers will often fail to recognize their creative contributions because they aren't artistic or aesthetic. An Engineer's work isn't necessarily pretty, but it works in a very Apollo 13-type of way.

5. THE HACKER

While the Artist often thrives in creating something new within the system, the Hacker is a little more subversive, actively working to tear down a broken system in order to create something better. In this sense, the Hacker is inherently destructive. However, this destruction nearly always serves a creative purpose: By turning systems upside down, the Hacker offers a new alternative.

Hackers are often the most misunderstood teachers in a school because people assume their sneaky non-compliance is somehow arbitrary or negative. What their accusers miss, though, is the fact that Hackers are often attuned to the quiet injustices kids face.

We once worked with a teacher who refused to follow certain rules. He thought it was silly that he had to post rules on the wall, so he posted them in five-point font on a notecard. He hated the fact that kids had to walk in a straight line to lunch, so he let kids walk how they wanted to walk and then said, "I was waiting for the line-based professional development. I've never walked in straight lines before, and I just don't feel confident in my ability to teach kids how to do this." When handing out test-preparation packets before a standardized test, he told kids to fill out whatever bubbles they wanted to fill out and race to the finish, so they could all read novels instead.

Many of this teacher's colleagues considered him to be a rebel who arbitrarily disobeyed the rules. They missed his heart for students. I (John) still remember a parent-teacher conference when a parent told me, "That man saved my life when I was in junior high. I was in a gang and hated school, and I told him that. He said, 'Me, too. I hate school. But I love learning.' Then he helped me learn to read."

Hackers don't always destroy systems. Often, they find new ways to use a system, idea, or resource. Think less "computer hacker" and more "life hacks." In these moments, the Hacker isn't fixing what is broken or creating something new so much as finding or designing a different, better way to use a current system. Here, the Hacker mashes things up in ways previously untried.

Sadly, in many systems, the Hacker is seen as destructive. People miss the creative work being accomplished because they have little tolerance for the divergent thinking that the Hacker offers. It's too bad, because Hackers are adept at keeping things fresh and pushing innovation in the least expected places.

6. THE POINT GUARD

Sometimes creativity involves making things. You build stuff. You design stuff. And you can touch it with your own two hands. But sometimes, the things you make aren't things at all. Sometimes you make a difference. You plan an event and people don't see it as creative because it's an experience rather than a product.

When you think of creative geniuses, chances are you imagine an artist or a designer before you think of an athlete. However, sports require exceptional creativity. The ability to see potential outcomes and patterns in various situations, for example, is crucial for a team's success. And one of the most creative positions in sports is the point guard in basketball.

A point guard is able to think differently in the moment and create opportunities as a result. Magic Johnson was unstoppable because he constantly and intentionally viewed the landscape of the court from different angles and set up opportunities that allowed the whole team to thrive. Similarly, Diana Taurasi dominated the WNBA by balancing passing and scoring, often setting up situations that opponents failed to anticipate.

The same creativity is required in the classroom. When a teacher takes the Point Guard approach, she thinks differently about the context and sets up new opportunities for students. The end result isn't a final product but an experience her students hadn't anticipated.

It's easy to miss the power of this creative approach because, at its best, it looks almost effortless. But it isn't. In fact, it's hard to pull off. You have to think on your feet, stay aware in the moment, and view the landscape from different perspectives. You must be part activist and part chess master.

THE KEY TO CREATIVE COLLABORATION

It's pretty common for people to identify with more than one type of creative approach. You might be a Geeky Artist or the Hacker-Engineer. That's totally normal. It's also appropriate to use different approaches depending upon the situation. Very few individuals, however, thrive using all of these approaches. That's why it's important to recognize the diversity and value of each one, particularly in schools, because schools need every type of creative teacher.

When schools embrace all types of creative teachers, we are able to build the kinds of learning environments our students deserve. Each type of creative teacher offers not only a new set of creative ideas but a different way of thinking. If every teacher is an Artist, schools will miss out on the chance to tweak systems, design structures, or hack what already exists. At the same time, when schools push data-driven decision making and focus on systems and structures, they miss out on the bold, blank-canvas ideas that the Artists in their midst can offer.

When we understand and appreciate the varied approaches to creativity, we are better able to embrace our differences and work in a way that is complementary rather than divisive. Artists need Engineers. Hackers need Geeks. The more we recognize and honor these differences, the better we are at designing creative classrooms.

We Are All Makers

In *An Astronaut's Guide to Life on Earth*, Chris Hadfield writes about one of the mindset problems of doing creative work:

> *In any new situation, whether it involves an elevator or a rocket ship, you will almost certainly be viewed in one of three ways. As a minus one: actively harmful, someone who creates problems. Or as a zero: your impact is neutral and doesn't tip the balance one way or the other. Or you'll be seen as a plus one: someone who actively adds value. Everyone wants to be a plus one, of course. But proclaiming your plus-oneness at the outset almost guarantees you'll be perceived as a minus one, regardless of the skills you bring to the table or how you actually perform.[1]*

Because we typically try to gauge our effectiveness and creativity in relation to the people around us, we tend to either overvalue or undervalue what each creative type brings to the table.

In his time at the helm of the International Space Station, Hadfield clearly saw that the ability to work well alone wasn't as important as the ability to recognize how each member of the team could work together. The whole was more than the sum of its parts: each individual's tasks, roles, and accomplishments. *Everyone* possesses important skills and talents, but it's only when we honor and tap into those skills and talents that we, together, can do exceptional creative work. In the next few chapters of this book, we'll look at the process that allows all creative types to work together toward a product, a solution, or an idea. We call this process the LAUNCH Cycle.

Visit TheLaunchCycle.com/mindset to get more information and resources on finding your Creative Approach. Join the discussion online using the hashtag #launchbook.

Notes

1. Chris Hadfield, *An Astronaut's Guide to Life on Earth*,(Little, Brown and Company, 2013).

CHAPTER 3
THE LAUNCH CYCLE

*Unleashing our inner creativity is like so many things
we try; the more we practice the easier it gets.*

**– Tom and David Kelley,
Authors of *Creative Confidence***

My (A.J.) newborn son lay quiet in the incubator at the hospital. It is a parent's worst nightmare to think something is wrong
with your child. I tried to keep it together, but even though my
face told the story of a calm, rational adult, my heart raced with
fear.

Worst-case scenarios flooded my mind and worry made each minute seem like an hour as I waited to learn of my child's fate.

My worries eased a bit when the doctor told me everything was going to be fine. Looking at my son through the nursery window, I saw peace on his face as the warmth from the incubator enveloped his tiny body. The miracle of a new life amazed me, but I missed the modern miracle of the incubator. My wife and I took for granted the $20,000 device that helps newborn babies survive the most dangerous beginning days of their existence. Yet, as we brought home my son a few days later, it came up in conversation with family and friends whose children also had to spend time in incubators as newborns.

Little did I know that more than four million premature or low-weight babies die each year primarily from hypothermia (when the body temperature drops below a healthy mark). I had spent time in South Africa and Swaziland and heard stories about infant mortality during the winter months, but I never connected the dots. It seemed that my child was healthy and happy because of a device our hospital could afford, while millions of parents around the world did not have that luxury.

Finding a way to provide affordable, life-saving equipment to hospitals and clinics in poor areas of the world is the exact problem a group of Stanford students took on during a 2007 project. Jane Chen, Linus Liang, Naganand Murty, Rahul Panicker, and Razmig Hovaghimian met in the "Design for Extreme Affordability" course at Stanford's d.school (Institute of Design). Their professor challenged them to design an invention for neonatal hypothermia that cost less than 1 percent of the price of a state-of-the-art incubator.

That semester this group of students came up with many ideas to solve the problem; however, almost every single idea involved an electric solution. It wasn't until the team visited Nepal that they became truly aware of the main issue: Rural areas did not have access to electricity, and many urban areas had sporadic electricity at best. Their solution, it seemed, could not involve plugs and cords.

By the end of the semester, the team had designed the first prototype: An infant warming blanket that was filled with heated margarine. Boiling water (used to heat the margarine) was the only requirement for the blanket to keep the baby warm for an extended period. Fueled by research and positive iterations, the team created a non-profit organization and continued to create prototypes and conduct research in 2008 and 2009. The project was no longer about a grade; it was about saving lives.

In March of 2010, Baby Nisha was born and became the first low-birth-weight infant enrolled in Embrace's clinical trial study at Cradle Hospital in Bangalore, India. By November, multi-center clinical trials began in three hospitals in India: St John's Hospital, Manipal Hospital, and Cradle Hospital. The testing of 155 newborns confirmed that the Embrace infant warmer was as effective as the current standard of care.

Finally, in April of 2011, the first Embrace infant warmer was delivered to a hospital in India. After four long years of inquiry, research, ideating, prototyping, creating, and launching, the team who met in a graduate school class had a product. The team had this to share about their journey:

We faced every challenge that could have possibly arisen in the days leading up to product launch, from a component of the product being stuck in customs, another not being delivered on time, to the wash tags being placed incorrectly. With an amazing team effort, we were ready to deliver our first product on April ninth.

Then, on the way to the clinic, we got a flat tire. Everyone in the car simply jumped out, piled into an auto rickshaw, and hand delivered the first unit to Little Flower maternity home. The experience was truly symbolic: no matter what obstacles we face (or how many flat tires we get), we'll find a way to reach our goals. It was an exhilarating feeling to deliver that first unit, knowing that we were one step closer to achieving our mission.[1]

Projects like Embrace show the power of design thinking to tackle any problem and come up with a creative solution. When you hear "design thinking," those words may conjure images of makerspaces and STEM labs. But design thinking is bigger than STEM. It begins with tapping into student curiosity and allowing them to create, test, and recreate until they eventually launch what they've made to a real audience (sometimes global, but often local).

WHAT IS DESIGN THINKING?

Design thinking isn't a subject, topic, or class. It's more a way of solving problems that encourages positive risk-taking and creativity. And when you start looking for examples of design thinking, you'll see it all over the place.

In the non-profit world, program designers use design thinking to develop solutions for the populations they serve. Engineers use design thinking to create tangible products. Meanwhile, authors have a more abstract approach as they work through the publishing cycle (which mirrors the design thinking cycle almost identically).

To understand design thinking, it helps to imagine it as the foundation and frame of a building. What type of building you create, what materials you use, how you decorate it, and where you build it is all tied to your unique personality. Want to build a house and decorate it with gold-colored macaroni art and velvet pictures of Elvis? Go for it. It's yours. Want to create a shop where you can sell chocolate-covered bacon? Go for it. The world can always use more bacon.

Another way to understand design thinking is to imagine a visit to your local frozen yogurt shop where you can choose whatever flavor you want and top it with whatever candy you want. (From our point of view, frozen yogurt is really just an excuse to eat candy and ice cream and call it "healthy.") The final product is distinctly yours. You were the one who decided mint yogurt and peanut butter cups would make a great combination. But even if the end product is unique, the process is common to everyone. Every customer pulled levers, added candy, and weighed their glorified sugar bomb.

The same is true of design thinking. Although the materials and finished products may vary widely (you might have a service project or a physical product, for example), the general process is common to everyone. Additionally, this process or framework is a cycle. Making is messy, and that's okay. However, without a framework, the mess remains simply that: a mess. The design thinking cycle actually boosts creativity by walking students through specific stages of the creative journey. Some of the most creative thinkers in the universe (don't tell the inhabitants on Naboo) follow this framework, and they see it as a way to open up new possibilities rather than a system that stifles their creative work.

It's important to note that researchers debate on the precise steps and the correct terminology for each stage in the design thinking cycle. Typically, design thinking follows the pattern of empathize, define, ideate, prototype, and test. However, we've added a few stages, including a phase for inquiry and a final phase for launching your creation to the world.

We also changed up the terminology to make it more kid friendly and memorable. We use the acronym LAUNCH to describe the cycle.

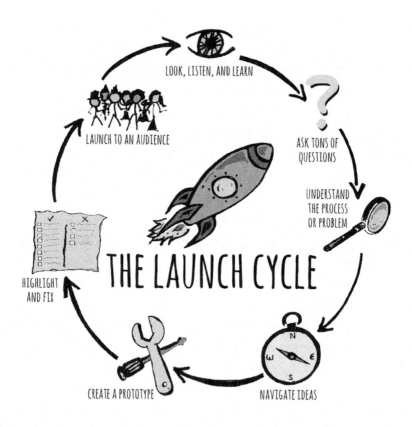

LOOK, LISTEN, AND LEARN

LAUNCH TO AN AUDIENCE

ASK TONS OF QUESTIONS

UNDERSTAND THE PROCESS OR PROBLEM

HIGHLIGHT AND FIX

THE LAUNCH CYCLE

CREATE A PROTOTYPE

NAVIGATE IDEAS

THE LAUNCH CYCLE

The following are the stages in the LAUNCH Cycle:

Look, Listen, and Learn

Ask Lots of Questions

Understand the Problem or Process

Navigate Ideas

Create

Highlight What's Working and Failing

Get ready to *Launch*!

Phase 1: Look, Listen, and Learn

Look, listen, and learn phase is all about awareness, which is where the whole process begins. Students see or experience something and become cognizant of an idea, a system, or an issue. It could happen when the teacher presents them with a scientific or engineering problem. Other times, that awareness dawns when they notice other people and their needs. Empathy kicks in and they start paying attention to a specific set of problems faced by a group of people. Still, other times, this phase starts with a simple sense of wonder or curiosity that ultimately leads to creative breakthroughs.

In the awareness stage, a teacher might have students do interviews, needs assessments, or observations to discover more about the challenge.

Phase 2: Ask Lots of Questions

As students grow more aware of an idea or an issue, they come up with questions. This can happen both individually and collaboratively. In this phase, students tap into their natural curiosity on the topic and, ultimately, land on a specific problem that needs to be solved. From there, they develop a set of questions they can use as they endeavor to understand the problem they are trying to solve.

In this phase, we often ask students to create questions individually, before pairing up and sharing their questions. Then they can participate in a group brainstorming session. Some students might need sentence stems or sample questions, and that's okay. Although inquiry is a natural human process, sometimes kids lack the language to articulate their curiosity. Sentence stems help students figure out how they can ask insightful questions.

Phase 3: Understand the Process or Problem

After asking questions, students move into research. Here is where they gain an understanding of the systems and key information connected to their problem. They might research causes and effects. They might do market research on a competing product. With a vague idea of how they want to solve the problem, they may do some research on how others have tried to solve it previously. The goal is for students to gather as much information as possible, so they can understand the problem and ultimately generate ideas for a solution (in the next phase).

In some cases, students conduct additional interviews and needs assessments to clarify their audience. Other times, they talk to experts on the subject. They will often access informational texts and find facts connected to their driving question. Or they might play around with a physical idea that they want to explore before actually creating anything.

The amount of structure you provide as a teacher is dependent on the needs of your class.

Phase 4: Navigate Ideas

Sometimes people call this phase "whiteboarding," and it is inherently messy and collaborative. After growing in their conceptual understanding, students have the chance to brainstorm and navigate multiple ideas until they can form a general plan. We usually break up this phase into a mini-cycle of open-ended brainstorming followed by an analytical process of picking apart the ideas and then moving back to brainstorming. After going through this phase, students have a clear idea or concept of what they will make.

When we asked students to create a metaphor for this process, the answers vary wildly. Some describe it as moving a camera around until they find the right scene or object for the frame and then gently shifting it into focus. Others describe it as moving all around on a trip before finally settling on a destination. Still others compare it to dumping a bunch of LEGO bricks on the ground (the brainstorm) and then sorting through them to decide what to build. None of the metaphors are perfect, but they all have this concept of being loose, chaotic, and open before zeroing in on a specific concept and shaping it into a specific idea.

Phase 5: Create

This is the stage in which students begin building their first model. It might be a video game created with Scratch (a popular programming tool) or the first draft of a digital magazine. However, it doesn't have to be techy. Some of the best creating involves cardboard and duct tape. Or it could involve writing a story, creating an event, or doing a service project.

This is the hands-on phase, where students take their ideas and turn them into a reality. Note that students will often want to jump straight into this phase and skip the previous four stages. However, creating the foundation ahead of time allows for a smoother and more focused process of creating.

Phase 6: Highlight and Revise

The Highlight and Revise phase works in a cyclical model where students determine what works and doesn't work and then change their prototype to try to resolve the glitches. The data they highlight can be quantitative and objective, like a bridge project, robotics project, or science experiment. But it can also be subjective and qualitative, as is the case with the peer feedback on a novel or a documentary.

In this phase, they should have a clear vision of what quality looks like and how they will assess it. After they've highlighted what's working and failing, they need extended time to go back and revise their prototype. These revisions will ultimately provide a chance to highlight what's working and not working again, then students may revise once more in an ongoing cycle until the product or plan is ready to launch.

Phase 7: It's Launch Time!

Eventually, students send their finished work to an authentic audience and attempt to convince people that their design is worth considering. As this happens, they get the chance to see if their idea is working. Does the audience like it? Are they using it?

This authentic feedback ultimately provides a chance to grow more empathetic with the user or audience, which leads back to awareness. When that happens, students can go through the cycle again with a focus on developing a 2.0 version or creating something entirely new.

Note that the design thinking cycle is not meant to be a formula that you follow rigidly so much as an approach to creativity. Think of it as something flexible and adaptable. Students might need to do some research while they create. They might bounce ideas back and forth before they've ever reached the navigating ideas phase. That's okay. To borrow the frozen yogurt metaphor, the yogurt flavor is far less important than the candy you add to it. Then again, we're almost always thinking about candy. *Mmm...*candy. And now you're thinking of candy.

BRAIN BOOST
STANFORD D.SCHOOL

One of the leading universities actively working with design thinking is Stanford. Specifically, Stanford d.school. Their website (dschool.stanford.edu) and companion K-12 site (k12lab.org) are both fantastic resources for educators at all levels. What we love about Stanford d.school is their approach to teaching and learning to focus on innovators, not innovations:

> At the d.school, we learn by doing. We don't just ask our students to solve a problem; we ask them to define what the problem is. Students start in the field, where they develop empathy for people they design for, uncovering real human needs they want to address. They then iterate to develop an unexpected range of possible solutions, and create rough prototypes to take back out into the field and test with real people.
>
> Our bias is toward action, followed by reflection on personal discoveries about process. Experience is measured by iteration: students run through as many cycles as they possibly can on any project. Each cycle brings stronger insights and more unexpected solutions.[2]

IS THE LAUNCH CYCLE RIGHT FOR MY CLASSROOM?

At first glance, the seven stages feel convoluted and time-consuming. You may even be thinking, "There's no way I'm going to be able to do this with student projects." What educators (including us) sometimes fail to notice is that students may need to go back and re-explore parts of this process that they might have missed on the first pass. A lack of research at the beginning may put them in a loop of trying and failing to solve problems. Without access to the right information, any progress they make will be slow. The lack of an Asking phase means that, even if they are doing the research by the book, their work is shallow and without authentic curiosity. The lack of a Look, Listen, and Learn phase means they probably don't have a strong sense of awareness.

In the long run, the LAUNCH Cycle actually saves teachers time. The structure simplifies the creative process by breaking it down into practical parts that students can actually accomplish. And the teacher can modify these individual parts to take as long as they need.

DESIGN THINKING MAY SEEM SLOW, BUT IT ACTUALLY SAVES TIME IN THE LONG RUN.

Can Design Thinking Work in All Subjects?

When I (John) taught self-contained, I had the chance to work with all subject areas. I found that design thinking worked really well in inquiry-driven science experiments (where it was less about prototyping and more about building an experiment and testing it) in writing (where there's already a sense of audience, brainstorming, writing, revising, and publishing) and in social studies.

I had a tougher time using this framework in math. It worked somewhat in math when we used Dan Meyer's visual prompts, leading into problem-solving, comparing, testing, and revising. However, the only time it worked really well in math was in our probability unit, where students designed board games from scratch using their knowledge of probability.

We might do well to look at the places where design thinking is already happening at school. For example, the design cycle works really well in journalism, yearbook, shop class, culinary, and theater, as well as in art and music. The common theme for all of these courses is that they are a natural fit for experimentation, trial, error, and discovery. Maybe it's time we integrate those attributes into the core subjects as well.

Can Design Thinking Work with All Ages?

Design thinking might seem like a framework aimed for secondary education, but it also works well in primary grades. Younger students are inherently inquisitive and aware, which naturally leads to the first two phases. It isn't difficult to tap into the sense of wonder with younger children. After all, they think bugs are *fascinating*.

Although younger students will need additional structure in the Understanding phase, they will love learning new information. If you, as a teacher, can bring in guests to act as primary sources, students can practice inquiry by simply asking questions. In terms of informational texts, there are often books written at younger levels and online resources that you can use for informational literacy. And technology provides endless information resources in video and multimedia formats.

Furthermore, younger students tend to thrive when navigating ideas and creating things. Watch them on the playground and you'll see students dreaming up new worlds, bargaining on roles, and reinventing games. Give them a cardboard box, scissors, and duct tape and watch them build something from scratch.

At first glance, it would seem that younger students might not have the patience for highlighting and changing their work. However, early childhood is packed with opportunities for incremental revision. Kids are used to making mistakes. Think about the process a child goes through to learn to ride a bike, speak a second language, or learn an instrument. Chances are they have a level of patience that rivals what most adults can handle. Seriously. These are the kids who, just a year or two before, were able to sit down and watch a full episode of *Dora the Explorer*. A little kid can handle tedium like a boss.

While the LAUNCH Cycle works with all ages, it's important to keep things developmentally appropriate. High school students tend to be more self-directed than early elementary. So scaffolding is important. Younger students often need more manipulatives and tactile interaction with the subject through the entire process. This is why we will include examples from all age groups throughout this book.

When Does It Work Best?

Given the long-term creative nature of design thinking, it can help to think about the ideal scenario for using it. It tends to work best in the following scenarios:

- **When students are making actual products** - We have had projects fail miserably because we went through the LAUNCH Cycle only to find that we didn't have the right materials to pull off a decent prototype. This happened when we used a vague "create-a-product" project and students wanted to design cars. We simply didn't have the materials to make things work. The key is to make a prototype possible in a tangible way, not only a conceptual idea.

- **When students have the time to go through the entire process (often larger projects)** - We've tried using the design thinking cycle in a two-hour block, and it was way too rushed. There's a time and a place for short creative works (a blog post, a forty-five-minute design challenge, a short video), but the LAUNCH process works best when students can devote significant time to their projects.

- **When you, as a teacher, have the freedom to allow this to work** - There's no getting around the fact that it's harder to spend significant time on large projects when you're in a high-stakes testing environment. However, in a future chapter, we'll be getting into some practical strategies for aligning design thinking projects to standards. We will also offer templates you can modify for communicating the design thinking cycle to stakeholders, such as parents, community members, and administrators.

- **With standards-based grading, where students can continue to revise in order to reach mastery** - Design thinking encourages creative risk-taking with the goal of eventual mastery. Unfortunately, traditional grading systems, where you average scores of assignments, fail to allow for revision and mastery. In contrast, a standards-based framework aligns well with design projects.

- **When the specific problem that students are solving is important to them** - This is why student choice and inquiry are critical early on in the process. There will be aspects of design projects that are tedious and difficult. Students will run into walls. However, when they care deeply about their work, they will be able to persevere in their creative process.

THE POWER OF THE LAUNCH CYCLE

Caine Monroy loved arcades so much that he decided to make one of his own. Limited to duct tape, packing tape, and tons of cardboard boxes, he began designing his own games. He would study how games worked and then navigate the ideas before creating the games and testing them out. As his father put it, "He loves to take things apart and see how things work. Can't put them back together, but he takes them apart."

WHAT YOU SEE:

WHAT A CHILD SEES:

Though Caine knew nothing about design thinking, he had uncovered the LAUNCH Cycle through this process of paying attention, asking questions, designing, building, and ultimately testing out his creations.

But there was a critical piece missing. He didn't have an audience. Although his dad had printed him a T-shirt with the words "Caine's Arcade," he was picked on at school for wearing it. And so his brilliant creativity had been limited to an audience of one. Each weekend, he would stand on the sidewalk with tickets and invite the few pedestrians nearby to play the game.

Then it happened.

A filmmaker named Nirvan Mullick happened upon the store on the last day of summer. What he saw blew him away—so much so that he organized a flash mob through social media and created a documentary. To Caine's surprise, a packed crowd gathered around his arcade to play the cardboard games he had created.

That was only the beginning. The short film went viral, and suddenly Caine had the chance to speak to large audiences and eventually give a TED Talk[3]. Caine and Mullick worked together to create the Imagination Foundation and the Global Cardboard Challenge.

Caine's Arcade dispels many of the myths we have about design thinking: that it requires tons of resources, that it works best with older students, or that it requires a state-of-the-art STEM lab. Note that Caine was young when he first began his cardboard arcade, but he wasn't too young to design games and modify them in an ongoing cycle. Notice, too, that his materials were limited. Caine didn't need a 3-D printer or a maker kit or access to the world's most comprehensive engineering software. If anything, the limitations in his environment and the freedom to experiment pushed him toward innovation.

Caine's Arcade shows not only the power of creativity but the power of an audience. Without a launch, Caine would have remained a lonely boy creating cardboard arcade games. With the flash mob and the viral video, Caine gained the confidence to be a leader. And what began as a project became a movement that has inspired educators all over the planet to do cardboard challenges and set up design projects.

Ultimately, the confidence they learn from launching is what we want for students. Not every one of them will launch a movement. But they can launch something. Not every one of them will build an amazing arcade. But they can all build something. If Caine's story proves anything, it's that creativity is deeply human and that the LAUNCH Cycle is a powerful way to design something that matters and share it with an authentic audience.

Visit TheLaunchCycle.com/cycle to get more information and resources (including digital posters) on the LAUNCH Cycle. Join the discussion online using the hashtag #launchbook.

Notes

1. http://Embraceglobal.org/who-we-are/our-story
2. http://dschool.stanford.edu/our-point-of-view/#innovators
3. Caine Monroy, "Outside the Box: Caine Monroy at TEDxTeen," Youtube.com/watch?v=kRCrAT1YcTo, March 27, 2013.

Chapter 4
Look, Listen, and Learn

Don't seek to be the best, seek to do your best.
- Sarah Thomas

Think about the products you use. It might be that bacon-covered donut you had for breakfast or that hideous puffy sweater your Aunt Gertrude bought you last winter. Those are physical products.

However, a product could also be the song you listened to during your prep period (you know, that one time when it wasn't taken up with meetings), the app that delivered the music, or the advertisements you had to listen to in order to stream that music for free.

The truth is that you are surrounded by stuff that was designed.

Some of these are intangible services while others are physical goods. Some of these are imminently practical while others exist for sheer entertainment. Regardless of the differences, every one of these products or services began with a specific design in mind.

Chances are, the design didn't begin with an epiphany. Whether it's artistic or practical, a service or a good, an artisan work or something manufactured by a large company, each product started with an idea. So where do the ideas come from? How do you help develop the right kind of product? Where do you begin when you can't figure out what you want to make? The LAUNCH Cycle offers an interesting perspective on the answers to those questions.

LOOK, LISTEN, AND LEARN

PHASE ONE: STARTING WITH AWARENESS

Many design thinking experts and enthusiasts label empathy as the first stage of design thinking. The idea is that designers should begin with a firm understanding of the audience. If you are eventually going to design a product, you start with a clear understanding of some kind of problem, need, or issue with which consumers are dealing. If you are going to write a book, you consider your audience before you write the first word. If you are writing a song, you have a clear picture of who will hear you perform it.

It makes sense to start with empathy. You want to make something your audience will use. However, after talking to designers in countless industries, we realize that a great design doesn't always begin with a specific audience in mind. An artist who feels the urge to create a work of art may not discover the audience until later. (For Vincent van Gogh, it was *much* later.) Curiosity and exploration may spark an idea. A creative work can begin when someone's natural sense of wonder is piqued about a phenomenon or system.

We put awareness at the starting point for Design Thinking because, while awareness can involve empathy for an external audience, it may also include (or stem from) a deeply personal awareness of a process, a system, or a phenomenon. Awareness can be scientific or artistic, social or economic, human centered or systems centered. Awareness can look different for each student in each class. In fact, we've identified seven ways to tap into student awareness.

SEVEN WAYS TO TAP INTO STUDENT AWARENESS

The process of establishing awareness will vary from project to project. It will look different depending upon the subject you are teaching, the mix of students that comprise the class, their age, and the final product you want them to create. It's important to realize that you can't make someone aware. Awareness isn't something *you* create in another person. It's a desire you have to tap into. However, you can construct scenarios to expand your students' awareness and increase their curiosity. Here are seven strategies you might want to use:

1: Start with the observation of a phenomenon.

Observation is a natural tool for math and science. Students see a specific phenomenon and they start growing in awareness. It might involve looking at magnets or plants. Whether they realize it or not, they will compare what they are observing with past observations. They might even tap into former observations they did in those really cool labs previously in your class. Sometimes, what they see will confirm what they know. Other times, new insights will challenge their preconceived notions of how the world works. Either way, they will grow more aware about the subject.

In the Look, Listen, and Learn stage, students might simply ask questions about what they are seeing and experiencing, or focus on data and trends. The process might not look inherently creative. Students are not likely to say, "I want to make something based upon this observation." (In fact, we can guarantee they won't use those words.) However, their wonder will lead to inquiry, then research, and eventually a product idea.

Teachers can tap into this wonder by providing hands-on experiences that allow students to play while they observe. You might even want to go on a field trip—or even a walk—away from the classroom. Alternatively, the phenomenon might be best observed with a set of manipulatives you use in the classroom. Or it might mean looking at an organism and sitting down with a sheet of paper and sketching it. Whatever approach you use to tap into your students' natural sense of curiosity, the key idea is engaging them in such a way that they become profoundly and deeply interested in what they are seeing.

Questions to Ask Your Students

- What do you see happening?

- What are you noticing?

- What questions come to mind as you observe this?

- What does this make you wonder?

- Is this interesting? Why or why not?

- Play around with it. Afterward, describe what it was like using the five senses.

Sentence Stems

- I am noticing that _____.

- I see that _____.

- I am seeing / smelling / hearing / feeling _____.

- I find it interesting that (describe what you see) because _____.

- One of the questions I have is _____.

- I find it odd that _____ happens when _____.

Classroom Example

After seeing the wonders of magnetism, students describe what trends they see. This leads to a series of inquiry questions that guide them in the research process. Eventually, they work on magnetic roller coasters, applying what they have seen and observed into a practical product.

2: Tap into natural wonder.

While similar to the previous approach, this strategy can be based on past or potential occurrences, rather than a current phenomenon. In other words, while the last option is all about seeing and experiencing a physical phenomenon firsthand, this place of natural wonder is based upon all of those unanswered questions that kids have about their universe. Why do leaves change colors? Or more importantly, why do boogers change colors? What's the tallest building in the world? How many packets of Jell-O would it take to fill up the Pyramids of Giza?

Children are naturally fascinated by the wonder of their world. Hang out with a four-year-old and take a tally of all the questions they ask. Unfortunately, schools are more often de-signed to help students answer questions rather than question answers. Students rarely have the chance to ask whatever ques-tion they have and go off on a rabbit trail to find the answers.

Initially, this idea doesn't seem deeply connected to design. After all, how would asking about mucus colors lead to product design? But when students can pursue these questions and find the answers, they often end up wanting to convey what they learned in a creative format. It might be a podcast or a video sharing the answer. It might even lead to an entirely new prod-uct idea inspired by their natural wonder about the world.

Think about how many "creative types" have been inspired by the wonder in their world? Artists often talk about things they noticed or the burning questions they had that ultimately led them to a creative work. Engineers have often described the way a particular curiosity led to a deeper understanding of a physical process. Now what if your students had the opportunity to explore and discover? Might they, too, become "creative types"?

Questions to Ask Your Students

- What are you curious about?

- What do you wish you were learning right now?

- What questions do you have about your world?

- If school didn't have any subjects and your only criterion was learning, what would you study right now?

- What is something you've always wanted to know? There are no wrong answers.

Sentence Stems

- I wonder why _____.

- I wonder how _____.

- I wonder what would happen if _____.

- I've always been curious about _____ because _____.

Classroom Example

Students start out with a series of questions that propel them into research. After researching, they work in the ideation stage and develop a way to convey the answer to a larger audience. This leads to a series of instructional videos, curiosity podcasts, and thematic blogs that connect to the students' original questions.

3: Start with awareness about a specific issue.

Design thinking is often associated with STEM or with the business world (because it is so similar to the product-market cycle). Remember, however, that awareness can lead to services rather than tangible goods. When students see something that breaks their hearts, their social awareness often leads to empathy, exploration, and potentially the development of a solution.

What we love about this awareness-building method is that students don't have to have a solution in mind at the beginning. They don't even have to have a deep sense of empathy with those who are affected by the issue. In many cases, they will develop both the conceptual understanding and the empathy toward those they serve as they explore the issue in the research phase. All they need at first is awareness that a particular issue exists and that they can be a part of the solution.

Questions to Ask Your Students

- What issue do you care about? Why?

- What is one thing you wish you could change about the world?

- What is the biggest issue facing our school? City? World?

Sentence Stems

- It bothers me that _____.

- One issue I care about is _____.

- One of the things that breaks my heart about the world is _____.

- I have noticed (name the issue or problem). I think this matters because _____.

- It tears me apart when _____ because _____.

- One of the biggest problems in our world is _____. This is important to me because _____.

- If I could change the world, I would _____.

Classroom Example

Students start with the question, "What would you change about your world?" From there, they develop inquiry questions about the causes and effects of specific issues. They interview community members and conduct needs-assessment surveys. This leads to the development of a specific service project and an advocacy piece that they create.

4: Start with empathy toward a specific group.

The difference between this approach and the one previous is that it begins with empathy toward a specific group. It tends to work best when students identify with the group on a personal level. For example, rather than simply caring about poverty, students are able to empathize with the poor because they have either experienced for themselves (or personally know who someone has) what it feels like to go hungry or to not have a place to call home. Personal experience connects them on a heart level to the issues that those living in poverty face. Over time, their experiences and empathy enable them to develop solutions that can benefit the poor.

Some of the best social solutions begin with a deep, humble respect for what specific populations are experiencing. I (John) noticed this when working for an urban, low-income school. My students knew about poverty because they had seen the way it impacted people they cared about. Though many of my students wouldn't have called themselves poor (in their minds, poverty meant literal homelessness), they knew it. They felt it. They saw how economic needs impacted the community. So when we created a service project, they were able to design a specific set of solutions that honored the dignity of those around them.

Empathy doesn't have to be connected to a social issue, though. Students can begin with empathy for a specific consumer market. When they are able to see a specific problem that a niche group is experiencing, they are then able to develop a product that meets a consumer need. Many entrepreneurs uncover ideas for new products by interviewing with people who are experiencing a common problem. As they seek to understand the attitudes, beliefs, emotions, and mindsets of their potential audience, they develop empathy. The product, then, is often even more valuable to the end user because it was created with real people in mind, rather than a theoretical market.

Questions to Ask Your Students

- Think of a particular group (athletes, parents, students, engineers). What is some kind of problem they seem to be facing?

- What are some of the groups in society that are facing injustice? What are some of the causes?

- Think of a group that is currently mistreated in your school, neighborhood, or city. What is that group? Describe what's happening.

- What is an audience that is underserved? What could you create that would benefit this audience?

Sentence Stems

- It seems that _____.

- When I talk to people who are experiencing _____, they mention _____.

- One issue a lot of people face is _____. This bothers me because _____.

- One small problem that _____ face is _____.

Classroom Example

In my (John) third year of teaching, I met up with a brand-new teacher, Javier Lucero, who later became a close friend. He and I shared a desire to have students serve the community. Although we were a Title One school and our students were often the recipients of charity, we wanted to empower them to serve their community from the ground up. One afternoon, I shared a list of service projects I wanted students to do. He shook his head. "Let the students decide. Let them begin with awareness. Let them do research and then plan the projects on their own." A few weeks later, he founded the Social Awareness Club, and I developed Project IMPACT. Together our middle school students started with social awareness and moved through the LAUNCH Cycle to serve our community. It was powerful because it began with their awareness, their questions, and their voice.

5: Start with a specific problem that needs to be solved.

The previous two approaches allow students to address social needs. In this approach, the focus is more product oriented. For example, when we do our *Shark Tank*-style projects, students begin with a specific consumer problem. The guiding question: "What is an annoying problem people face today?"

Unlike the previous approach, we start with the problem rather than the group. Students aren't conducting interviews with future consumers. They're not trying to figure out who will use what they create. Instead, they look at the specific problem and make sure they have a clear picture of why it matters.

With a problem identified, we move into specific groups. "How does this problem affect kids? Parents? Teachers? Athletes?" By moving into this phase, students become aware of a specific problem and how it impacts a particular audience.

Questions to Ask Your Students

- What is an annoying problem that people are facing? Why is it a problem?

- What is something you wish you could create to make the world better?

- What kind of product do you wish you could make? What problem would it solve?

Sentence Stems

- I wish I could make a _____ because
  _____.

- If someone created a _____ then it would fix the problem of _____.

- One of the biggest problems we see is _____. This is an issue because _____.

Classroom Example

Students examine a specific consumer need. They delve deeply into questions about this problem with an emphasis on why it matters. Next, they explore the causes and effects of their core issue along with market research about other solutions that exist. Their newfound awareness ultimately leads to ideating and prototyping a specific product that they launch to a *Shark Tank*-style team.

6: *Start with a product idea.*

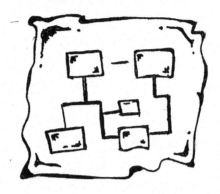

Sometimes awareness begins with a product idea. You might set out a specific challenge for your class to write a novel, create a blog, or film a documentary. This is the idea behind the National Novel Writing Month (NaNoWriMo). Students have a clear picture of the finished product in mind and then engage in research, work on the ideation, and build prototypes. However, in this very first stage, they aren't thinking about a problem, an audience, or a process. Instead, they are simply psyched out about making a product.

A word of caution here: If you start out with a general product in mind, keep it general. When students zero in on a specific idea without going through the research or ideation phases, they short-circuit the process and miss out on the chance to create something different. Starting off general can be difficult for students to figure out. For example, in the case of a novel, students might say, "I want to make a book about a sixth-grade kid who is a ninja." However, in the research phase they might look into other books that are out there and find that the concept has already been explored in-depth in *Diary of a Sixth-Grade Ninja.*

Teachers can help students remain flexible in their thinking by sharing examples of products that began as one idea but ended up with a totally different concept in the end. One strategy is to have students generate a list of multiple ideas ahead of time. Another strategy is to have them create a mash-up of multiple ideas. Or they could take an idea and figure out how they could improve it. A final strategy is to have students critique certain products (e.g., books, blogs, movies) and list what criteria make that product awesome or horrible.

Questions to Ask Your Students

- What are the types of _____ that you enjoy? What makes them so great?

- What kind of _____ doesn't exist but should?

- If you could improve _____, what would you do to change it?

- When you think of great _____, what are some of the things you notice?

- What criteria would you have for a great _____?

Sentence Stems

- I would like to create a _____ because _____.

- _____ would be better if we just _____.

- I think it would be cool to invent a _____, a _____, and a _____.

Classroom Example

In the NaNoWriMo project, students begin with a clear concept of the product parameters. They brainstorm possibilities and then shift into research, where they conduct market research on the originality of the idea. (With younger students this might be a visit to the library along with the creation of a short chapter book.) They might even research their story's setting. Afterward, they ideate in the form of webs, graphic organizers, and character sketches. Then they begin the proto-typing by writing the book.

7: Start with a geeky interest.

Design doesn't have to begin with a bold idea, empathy with an audience, or a clear understanding of a problem. It can simply start with a geeky interest. With initiatives like 20% Time and Genius Hour, students have the freedom to tap into their passions and interests and eventually apply their knowledge to a larger product. The benefit of this approach is that it supports intrinsic motivation through student choice. Moreover, it allows students to feel understood and affirmed while they tap into their prior knowledge. So you have a student who is into crocheting or unicorns or ninjas? Let them begin with what they love. Creative projects are inherently challenging (especially in the research phase). However, when students can begin with their own geeky interests, they can persevere.

Questions to Ask Your Students

- What do you geek out about?

- What are you most interested in?

- What are the things you would study in school if you were free to choose your focus?

- What would you love to learn if you could learn any-thing?

Sentence Stems

- I want to learn about _____ because _____.

- I've always been into _____ because _____.

- I wish I could learn more about _____ because _____.

Classroom Example

In our CuriosityCast podcasts, students start with a question they want to answer. This leads to research online. If you have connections, they might even get the chance to interview an expert in the field. After answering the question, they plan out their podcast and then record it, edit it, and launch it.

WHEN STUDENTS MAKE AWARENESS THE PRIORITY

"Is this real, Mr. J?" The question came from the back of the room. Todd rarely spoke up in class, but today he seemed visibly upset.

"Yes, it is real," I said. "Sadly, this type of thing is all too common around the world."

"But," Todd responded, "if this is going on right now, why doesn't the UN or someone go in there and stop it? Isn't that the reason we have all of these organizations … to stop this?"

Multiple students were raising hands now, eager to share their thoughts on what they had just seen. It was the first time I had shown my tenth-grade students the "Invisible Children: Rough Cut" documentary, and they wanted answers. The documentary followed a group of three young adults who ventured to Africa and saw the injustices of child warfare firsthand.

"Well," I said, "let me ask all of you a question before we go further into what we just watched. How many of you knew this type of human rights violation was happening *right* now in the world we all live in?"

Not one student raised a hand. The room was silent.

"Don't you think," I continued, "that is part of the problem? Don't you think that everyone would make this a top priority if they knew about this problem? Don't you think it would be on every news channel around the world, until something was done to end violence against children?"

After a few more seconds of silence, Kelly, an outspoken student, finally said, "Yeah, it would be all over the news, and we would all know about it, if it was happening in the US."

"I think you're right, Kelly. And I also think that is an awful truth. So what should we do about it?"

And that was the moment my students decided enough was enough. They CHOSE to tell the world about the human rights violations happening right now in their world by creating a powerful awareness campaign.

Students Choosing to Start a Movement

I've heard many of the same types of questions, over and over, when talking about student ownership and choice in the classroom:

- How can you keep students accountable?

- What if they don't do anything with their time?

- Does it connect to the standards?

- My curriculum is set; how can I do it?

- This doesn't seem possible in a class of twenty-five students.

And yet my tenth-grade classes, where the students launched a powerful awareness campaign during the year, were between twenty-five and thirty students each. The students kept one another accountable in groups. They went above and beyond anything we had written in our curriculum—and hit more standards than with any other project or activity we'd ever done.

Why?

Because they chose to help create a project they cared about.

After our discussion about human rights violations, child soldiers, and the genocide that was currently happening in our world right now, my students wanted to DO something.

We had recently read *Night* by Elie Wiesel as a class. The quote below from Holocaust survivor and political activist Elie Wiesel guided our campaign to create awareness about human rights violations:

> *I swore never to be silent whenever and wherever human beings endure suffering and humiliation. We must always take sides. Neutrality helps the oppressor, never the victim. Silence encourages the tormentor, never the tormented .*

As a class, we decided to not be bystanders. We decided to take a side and take a stand. This new project was the chance to use our voice to spread awareness.

Traditionally during this unit, my students would write a position paper on the Holocaust and genocide in general. Additionally, they'd send a letter to a senator about a current human rights violation.

That year, my students wanted to take their efforts further. Together, we crafted a new project that focused on creating awareness about current human rights violations. I say *we* because the students had a lot of input into how this project would look, what they would be measured on, and what the ultimate goals and objectives would be.

BRAIN BOOST
STUDENT-CENTERED LEARNING IN ACTION

Aside from all the good that was accomplished through this project, it also allowed me to see what student-centered learning actually looks like in the classroom. Take a look at the definition of student-centered learning below. I think you'll agree that Project: Global Inform models this powerful approach to education:

> Student-centered learning (SCL), or learner-centeredness, is a learning model that places the student (learner) in the center of the learning process. In student-centered learning, students are active participants in their learning; they learn at their own pace and use their own strategies; they are more intrinsically than extrinsically motivated; learning is more individualized than standardized. Student-centered learning develops learning-how-to-learn skills such as problem-solving, critical thinking, and reflective thinking. Student-centered learning accounts for and adapts to different learning styles of students (National Center for Research on Teacher Learning, 1999).[1]

Terms like student-centered learning can get a bad rap as buzzwords. But the truth is, I want my own kids to experience the type of learning that is defined in the above paragraph. I don't care if it is a buzzword or not; I only care about the actual work they are doing and how they feel about it.

What Awareness Looks Like in Project-Based Learning

Project: Global Inform (PGI) was created in the 2008–2009 school year at Wissahickon High School. The students picked their own groups and researched current human rights violations. Each group chose a violation they felt particularly passionate about and developed a plan for bringing the social injustice to the public's attention. Putting their plans into action, the students then evaluated how effectively each method of media spread information and created awareness. At the end of Project: Global Inform, the students had shared their messages with thousands of teens and young adults who witnessed media campaigns designed to create awareness.

In 2009–2010, Wissahickon High School took Project: Global Inform to almost the entire tenth-grade class. Hundreds of students created video, Web, and Facebook campaigns. Many student groups pulled together to host events to support the cause. The students collected thousands of dollars and put the project on the map, along with their chosen human rights violations.

Project: Global Inform was one of my proudest accomplishments as a teacher. It still gives me chills when I think about what these fifteen- and sixteen-year-old students did to spread awareness on such serious violations. The project's real-life results are an example of what can *really* happen in our schools when we give students choice and ownership of their learning experience.

The next time you do a project or activity in your class, ask these questions for your own awareness:

- What is each student's attitude toward learning?

- Is their commitment to the activity based on external or internal factors?

- Are students creating their own measures (goals/objectives) for achievement?

- Are they reflecting on how well they have achieved those goals/objectives, and what could be done differently?

During Project: Global Inform, students filled out an action plan template to decide as a group what their goals would be and also what their evidence of success would be.

ACTION PLAN TEMPLATE

Action Step: What will be done?	Responsibilities: Who?	Timeline: When will it be done? Day/month?	Resources: What do we have? What do we need?
Step 1: Planning			
Step 2:			
Step 3:			
Step 4:			
Step 5:			
Step 6:			
Step 7:			
Step 8:			
Step 9:			

Download a copy of the action plan template here:
TheLaunchCycle.com/action

Many groups "failed" to reach some of the lofty goals they set for themselves during this project. But each one of these groups presented to the class about their journey and spoke of how much they had learned, even if they did not reach a specific goal. It was the first time I had heard students talk about "failure" in a positive light; they realized that creating big goals gave them the opportunity to fail forward.

Have you experienced that moment where your students show you something about teaching and learning that you never knew could actually exist? Through Project: Global Inform my students used their awareness muscles to look, listen, and learn about human rights violations around the world. They then turned the project into a community-wide awareness campaign, and in doing so made me realize what happens when you take the shackles off learning and let your students create, make, and publish with passion.

Visit TheLaunchCycle.com/look to get more information and resources on Phase 1 of the LAUNCH Cycle. Join the discussion online using the hashtag #launchbook.

Notes

1. http://ccliconference.org/files/2010/03/Froyd_Stu-CenteredLearning.pdf

Chapter 5
Ask Tons of Questions

Inquiry. It's not a new idea.

- Joy Kirr

Imagine being a child and listening to a teacher talk, but instead of a normal flow of speech, the teacher's words have a slight delay, like the lag that sometimes happens when you're streaming video. That lag is annoying enough when you're trying to binge watch your favorite show, but what if every word you heard was delayed?

At best, every single conversational moment would be an incredible nuisance. At worst, the potential misunderstandings could put you at a disadvantage.

OFTEN THE LABELS KIDS RECEIVE BECOME THE LIES THAT THEY BELIEVE.

This is Scott Barry Kaufman's reality. At three years old, doctors discovered Scott had an auditory processing disorder that made it almost impossible for him to understand words in real time. When Scott was just nine years old, his school tested him using an IQ test for intelligence. Unable to follow what the test administrator was saying during the test, he struggled to answer the questions and received an extremely low score.

Next thing you know, the school labeled Scott a "special education" student and assigned him to the school "resource room" where he was separated from classmates during instruction. The label had nothing to do with his actual cognitive abilities or his hearing disability; it instead was based on his IQ test results.

As Scott puts it, when you are a kid and an adult tells you how smart you are (or aren't), you tend to believe that person. The special-education label put young Scott on a slow track that he stayed on until he reached ninth grade. Thankfully that year, a teacher named Joyce Jeuell saw something the test had missed. She noticed that he was bright and capable of far more than what the resource room offered him. One day, Joyce pulled Scott aside and asked, "Why are you still in the resource room?"

That one question started Scott on a path of personal discovery. He asked a ton of questions about his label, his place in school, and what kind of learning experience he could (and should) be having. Those questions and the answers he found changed the course of his life.

What's Scott doing today? Let's take a quick look at where all those questions led him in his schooling and career.

Scott earned a PhD from Yale in cognitive psychology, has worked as a professor at New York University, and currently runs the Imagination Institute at the University of Pennsylvania. He is the best-selling author of *Ungifted: Intelligence Redefined* and writes a column in *Scientific American* in his free time.

Wow.

ASK TONS OF QUESTIONS

PHASE TWO: ASK TONS OF QUESTIONS

Scott's story is a bold reminder of the power of inquiry and wonder. Initially, the system didn't know what to do with him—especially when he began asking questions and challenging his label. Because he didn't fit the mold of a compliant child, they shamed him. They were unable to see the creative potential and wild imagination beneath his barrage of questions.

It would be easy to look at Scott's story and view it as an exception. After all, not every child is naturally gifted. But here's the thing: Although not every child is gifted, every child has gifts. Not every child will create an Imagination Institution, but every child has a wild imagination. Every child is born with a natural curiosity. It is not something we have to teach, but it is something we must cultivate and nurture.

In design thinking, we embrace this sense of wonder and curiosity. When students reach a state of awareness in the Look, Learn, and Listen stage, they naturally begin to ask questions. This second stage will ultimately fuel the understanding that takes place in the third phase. These questions are the bridge that links awareness and research.

We want to see kids asking tons of questions. In fact, we are convinced that this is where learning begins.

IT ALL BEGINS WITH WONDER

IT ALL BEGINS WITH WONDER.

A few years ago, I (John) had the chance to teach science in a self-contained classroom (teaching all subjects). I scoured the Internet for examples of great demonstrations that would captivate my students' attention. It worked at first. I did the typical experiments. You know, add baking soda to vinegar. Pop some Mentos in Diet Coke. Get a hard-boiled egg to fall into a jar. That sort of stuff.

It was pretty cool, and for a short time, my demonstrations intrigued the students. However, the only thing my students learned in the process was that their teacher could replicate experiments that he had found online in a classroom. I upped the ante a week later by doing a few experiments first and having students follow directions to do the same. It was good, but we were all still just following directions.

My students were supposed to be learning how to think like scientists, but all they had learned was how to think like me. They hadn't owned the learning because they hadn't owned the process. They hadn't owned the questions. They hadn't engaged in any real creative thinking.

That evening when I drove home, I emptied the dishwasher while my three-year-old son bombarded me with questions. *Why does the sky turn orange on only some nights? Why does the moon show up in the day on some days and not others? What would happen if someone ate poop?* The last question was admittedly disturbing but, thankfully, he hadn't done any experiments to test the question—yet.

Later, I watched him running around the backyard, filled with wonder at everything he was experiencing. He naturally shifted from looking and listening into asking. Why did some bugs jump and others fly? What made the whiffle ball move funny? What made bubbles change colors? Why were some bubbles bigger than others? It struck me that this sense of wonder and wild curiosity is where real science begins. This barrage of questions was precisely what I wanted to hear from my students.

So I changed things up. The next day, I invited students to think like a three-year-old.

"Go on. Write down whatever questions you want to know about the physical world. There are no stupid questions. Seriously. Have at it."

My students struggled at first.

"Is this the right kind of question?" a girl asked.

"Is it a question?" I asked.

She shook her head.

"And it connects to the physical world?"

She nodded.

"Then it's perfect."

The questions covered a massive range of topics:

- Why does water suck when there aren't any clouds inside? (Then, in parentheses, the student wrote, "I think the word is evaporating.") Where does that water go if not in the clouds?

- Is it true that you can't drink a whole gallon of milk in an hour?

- Would you die if you drank Diet Coke and downed a pack of Mentos in the same minute?

- What makes stuff float? Why do certain heavy things not sink but light things sink?

- Why does metal always seem cold in a classroom if it's been in the same room temperature? Is it really getting colder? Or does it just feel that way?

- What makes paper airplanes fly faster?

- What makes the ripples in water?

- Why does stuff burn when it's together but not when it's apart?

- Why do some chemicals burn green and others turn red or orange?

- Why does it smoke afterward when you mix vinegar and baking soda together? Is that really smoke?

- Can a person really "blue flame" or is that an urban legend?

- If you kept a species of lizard in a totally yellow container, would the color change after years in that environment, even if there was nothing to force natural selection? I mean, if you had a room and all the lizards were normal, would they turn yellow in twenty years? Or a hundred years? Or never?

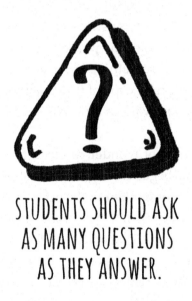

STUDENTS SHOULD ASK
AS MANY QUESTIONS
AS THEY ANSWER.

The questions varied in practicality and in understanding of science. There were certainly questions we couldn't pursue (burning chemicals or "making lizards evolve" or eating tons of Mentos and drinking Diet Coke or attempting to blue flame by farting into a Bunsen burner). However, as students narrowed down the questions, they moved into understanding the topic, navigating ideas, and ultimately creating an experiment.

It wasn't pretty. It was loud. It was messy. It was fun—kind of. Actually, the students felt frustrated half the time and then excited the other half. But in the process, they were engaged. They were thinking creatively about science.

Asking tons of questions launched us into a deliberate, forceful embrace of a state of wonder in the classroom. On other occasions, I had students look at different kinds of species and study them. That slow, deliberate act of observation was a different form of wonder. It was a slower, quieter curiosity, but it was just as powerful.

There's something disarming about starting with a sense of wonder in a design project. It doesn't feel so difficult to think about a specific audience or a really important product when you come at it with curiosity rather than the feeling that you have to know all of the answers or have the perfect idea. In some cases, students in this phase might not even know that they will be making something in the end. Even without an understanding of the full scope of the project, by asking questions they are becoming aware of a problem they will solve in their design.

A general sense of wonder can lead to bigger things. Note how many artists began not by thinking about an audience, but by having a sense of wonder in the act of making art. Note how many engineers began not by solving challenging problems, but by marveling at the wonder of the world around them. Note how many service projects began not by a desire to change the world, but by a justice-fueled curiosity about a particular problem (*I wonder why there is hunger. What I can do about it?*).

NARROWING DOWN YOUR QUESTIONS

Phase Two of the LAUNCH Cycle is all about getting as many questions out in the open as possible. We often begin by telling students, "You know how teachers tell you that there are no stupid questions? Well, the only stupid question in a design project is 'Should I ask this question?' Because even a seemingly stupid question is a chance to learn."

We explain that some of the best inventions began with a "stupid" question about combining two seemingly different ideas. A vague, half-baked idea often sparks the innovation that shakes the status quo.

It takes a certain amount of bravery to ask questions—especially when those questions seem silly or challenge the presuppositions of the crowd. If a student asks a basic question that "everybody knows," that student is admitting ignorance. But here's the thing: sometimes it's the crowd that's ignorant.

SOMETIMES THE BRAVEST THING YOU CAN DO IS ASK A QUESTION

I (John) remember a moment last year when my seventh graders were taking the laptops out in the morning.

"Mr. Spencer, why are the laptops so ... I mean ... what if they ..." he cut himself off before finishing.

"Go ahead. What are you wondering?"

He shook his head. "I'm sure we learned this in science."

"What?"

"Why are the laptops so cold? But then it has me wondering, like, what if the laptops aren't actually cold? What if they just *feel* cold?"

The kids around him laughed. A few of them felt the aluminum. "Dude, they're cold because they've been in a cart all night."

"But the tables were in the same room, right?"

This led to an impromptu exploration into thermal conductivity. This student spent the next ten minutes researching why metal feels colder than the air around it. The results were shocking. Often objects "felt" warmer or colder than their true temperature. This might seem like a simple lesson in chemistry, but for students it was mind blowing.

In many respects, uninhibited questioning comes more naturally to younger students. After all, they haven't learned that certain questions are "stupid." I remember visiting a kindergarten class during a prep period. It was amazing how many questions students asked. That same day, I watched my own students and noticed that, even in an inquiry-based project, many of them were reluctant to ask questions. I had to build in more opportunities to ask questions.

Creative classrooms are the ones where students are able to question answers as often as they answer questions. When we encourage students to ask their own questions, they get the chance to own the entire learning process. It's empowering. The result is more engaged learners who are more excited about the subject. In the process, they become the kind of lifelong learners that we want them to be.

But what happens when they struggle to ask questions? What happens when this very natural curiosity is somehow missing?

HOW DO WE HELP STUDENTS ASK BETTER QUESTIONS?

My students sit silently at their tables as I (John) wander through the still room. To an outside observer, the class appears orderly. But that's on the outside. Behind the intense eyes, thirty minds are running wild. They're tapping into their natural curiosity and jotting down the questions on notebook paper. It's low-tech. It's unassuming. But don't be fooled. It's powerful.

Ten minutes later, I call students to their groups and they share their thought-provoking questions. It's part of their video-game-design project. Suddenly, the room is filled with the sound of students bouncing questions back and forth in a sort of mental ping-pong game. They ask vague, abstract questions along with specific, fact-based research questions. They make inferences. They connect ideas from different systems. They ask clarifying questions to their group members. It's a messy process, but it's a beautiful kind of mess. It's art.

But it doesn't start this way. At the beginning of the year, my students struggle with inquiry. They aren't used to asking questions in class. However, over the course of the semester, they embrace inquiry. Here are some of the strategies you can use:

1. **Question everything.** Make this your mantra! As long as a question is respectful, allow students to question their world. This applies to analyzing mathematical processes, thinking through social issues, making sense out of a text, or analyzing the natural world for cause and effect. Every lesson should include students asking questions to you, to one another, or to themselves—and the boldest of students will ask questions of the world through social media and personal interviews.

2. **Do Wonder Days.** The idea is simple. Students begin with their own question and they research it, summarize it, and then ask further questions. Even if your initial goal involves teaching bias, loaded language, and summarization, you'll soon see how Wonder Days help students improve their ability to ask critical thinking questions.

3. **Give feedback on questions.** Students highlight one another's questions in Google Docs and leave comments on their blogs with very specific feedback. It might sound harsh, but it doesn't have to be. When all questions are being analyzed, students learn to write

things like, "This question is deep, but it's worded in a way that elicits a short answer response. Can you change it so that you draw a longer response?"

4. **Model the process.** Model the types of questions that require deeper thinking. This can happen during read-alouds as well as during class discussions. You can even ask a really lame question and then say, "Someone tell me why that question stunk." Or ask a deeper question: "Why was that a hard question to answer?" The goal is to get students to see deeper questions and to also think about why a question is deep or shallow.

5. **Practice it often.** Go beyond the LAUNCH Cycle to have students ask tons of questions. We do mock interviews, fake press conferences, and rotating discussion zones in the first week of school. Instead of spending time on ice breakers or excessive time on procedures, we spend time on learning to ask better questions.

6. **Spend more time playing.** Seriously. Wonder is something we can both encourage and allow in schools, and it often begins when we promote playing. It's sad that younger students are the only ones who get blocks of playtime. Is it any wonder that younger kids are more likely to ask random questions? Include blocks of time in your day to allow students to play, explore, and discover.

7. **Provide support.** Some students have a really hard time with questioning strategies. Providing sentence stems gives them a starting point. We understand if you don't like the idea of helping students form their question. Perhaps you believe (like we once did) that students can and should naturally ask questions and grow through accessing prior knowledge. Over time,

we've come to understand that language acquisition can be a barrier in asking better questions. Sentence stems and sample questions help young students and English-language learners (ELL) modify questions and access the language.

8. **Explain and model the different types of questions.** Teach students about clarifying, critical thinking, and inference questioning. The process may be messy with moments of overlap, but it helps students when they can think, "What needs to be clarified?" or "How does this relate to life?" From there, they can develop better questions.

9. **Embrace student choice.** It's difficult to generate questions when you don't really care about the subject. If you don't care about cars, you might think that the only difference between a Mustang and a Lamborghini is that one of them is easier to spell. But to someone who loves cars, a car is a work of art. And a student who is into cars will have an easy time creating tons of questions about cars.

10. **Use multiple grouping options.** Students will sometimes ask you questions. Other times they can ask partners or small groups questions. Additionally, they can ask the questions of the whole class. Then, when they do an article summary, they start with individual questions but eventually move into leading a whole-class discussion. This constant integration of multiple grouping creates a climate in which your students are always asking questions.

11. **Slow down.** I remember as a child feeling a sense of amazement at the ability to pull iron out of sand. We pulled out magnets and stuck them in all kinds of soil

until it worked. The process was slow. We weren't hurried. But this was precisely what led to inquiry. Often, these relaxed moments of wonder are precisely what students need to ask deeper inquiry questions.

12. **Follow rabbit trails.** When I was a pre-service teacher, my mentor said something so often it became a mantra for me: "We must seize the moment of excited curiosity for the acquisition of wisdom." He wasn't sure where the saying originally came from, but the idea was that in that single moment when your curiosity is sparked, you should chase it. If you put it off until later, you miss something in the process. Those questions evaporate. But when you chase the curiosity, you end up asking better questions and learning more in the process.

13. **Share your own questions.** A teacher who's naturally curious infects the entire classroom. Students love to hear their teachers say, "I'm trying to figure out _____," or "I've been exploring _____." Their curiosity meant that it was okay for me to be curious. You can give your students that same gift: the permission to wonder. When you talk about your own curiosity and you share the questions you have, you create a class culture that values inquiry.

14. **Reduce the fear.** Often when a student says, "I don't know what to ask," what they're really saying is, "I'm afraid of sounding stupid." If students have had to spend most of their time getting the questions right, it can feel unnerving to be told that they can now ask their own questions.

BRAIN BOOST
THE ART OF ASKING A GOOD QUESTION

You can't expect to wake up one morning and run a marathon without training. Similarly, asking good questions is a skill that requires practice, training, and mentoring. If a child (or adult) is placed in an environment that does not encourage active questioning, then that skill will not become an active habit of mind.

> *The purpose and practice of active questioning has its roots in ancient philosophic traditions. Socrates is well known for using questioning to probe the validity of an assumption, analyze the logic of an argument, and explore the unknown. Questions were a means to educate his students by drawing out their understanding of a subject and then leading them to discover a set of logical conclusions instead of lecturing them on what is true or false. Socratic questioning is still advocated as a powerful contemporary teaching method (Brill and Yarden, 2003).[1]*

WHAT DOES THIS LOOK LIKE?

At the Anastasis Academy in Denver, Colorado, students are asking their own questions. It's a bold experiment in inquiry-based learning. Here there are no grade levels, no subjects, no age levels, and no firm objectives for each lesson. Students receive feedback instead of grades.

"We begin with themes and let students ask their own questions," explains teacher Michelle Baldwin.

Often, these questions lead into larger design projects. Students in Baldwin's class have designed a golf course, a space station, and a model city. Their teacher works as a facilitator, providing materials and designing situations that will spark wonder. However, the students guide the journey, following their own questions and ultimately building what they want with the materials they choose. So that model city is an in-person model government with one group, a physical model in another group, and a second world in Minecraft.

"You never know where it will end up," Baldwin explains. "At one point, students became interested in the Mars Rover and ended up Tweeting with an astronaut and talking to engineers. In a connected world, they are able to access experts in ways that were once unthinkable."

Even in an open environment, she explains there are times when students check out and she has to guide them back to their original questions. It isn't a utopia, after all. Sometimes, freedom can be a difficult adjustment. However, those are a part of the learning process. As students experience more freedom, they grow self-directed and learn the art of project management.

It's a counterintuitive element of design thinking. The more slack we provide students, the more they become responsible. The freedom of inquiry doesn't lead to laziness but rather ownership.

"You cannot empower students to be self-directed, responsible, critical-thinking people if they can't ask their own questions. At that point, you're teaching compliance rather than responsibility."

You might be thinking, "That's great at Anastasis, but I teach in a school with firm policies about grading and standards."

That's okay.

Even at Anastasis, teachers vary on how they provide structure for inquiry. But what Michelle Baldwin's class proves is that student inquiry works and that it works in every subject with every age group. When students can ask their own questions, they get a chance to own the entire process.

Ultimately, that's what we want. We want students to be independent thinkers. We want them to be lifelong learners. We want them to be makers. And that all begins by allowing students to ask their own questions.

Visit TheLaunchCycle.com/ask to get more information and resources on Phase 2 of the LAUNCH Cycle. Join the discussion online using the hashtag #launchbook.

Notes

1. Vale, Ronald D. "The Value of Asking Questions." Ed. Keith G. Kozminski. Molecular Biology of the Cell 24.6 (2013): 680–682. PMC. Web. 16 Apr. 2016.

CHAPTER 6
UNDERSTANDING THE INFORMATION

Every child deserves someone to be crazy about them!
- Principal El,
Author of *The Immortality of Influence*

My (A.J.) daughter had been singing for almost two hours with no break. The song "Do You Want to Build a Snowman" from the Frozen soundtrack was on repeat.

My wife and I looked at each other. "She's pretty good," we both said as she added a new piece of choreography to her accompanying dance.

In fact, my mind started running about how good she really was, and how great she could become. *We all want the best for our own kids and our students.*

In my daughter's case, we made sure she had a variety of experiences trying new things. From T-ball and soccer, to swimming and gymnastics, my wife and I watched and supported her along the way.

But this was different. We always knew she liked singing and dancing, but now it had taken on a whole different level. I wondered if my daughter had found her first "passion."

Chances are you've been in this same spot as a parent or teacher. We give our kids a lot of opportunities, and when they finally find one they enjoy, we are excited by the possibilities. Sometimes parents and teachers may try to guide a child down a certain path of sports, music, or learning based on their interests, but usually we wait for that spark of passion to come; and when it does, the big question is, "What's next?"

Research. That may sound boring, but this phase is actually fascinating.

CHILDREN ARE ALREADY RESEARCHING BEFORE THEY EVER LEARN HOW TO READ.

Understanding the Information

Let us explain. When we think about research, we tend to have an idea in our mind of a library, tons of old books, and hours spent reading and searching for a clear-cut answer. But research doesn't have to look like a graduate student's nightmare; it can look like a child's daydream. Here's the truth that we tend to miss when discussing research:

Little kids research the world, even before they know how to read.

In my daughter's case, we saw the need to research after she started asking a ton of questions. She asked us things like:

- Who is really singing if Elsa's character is animated?

- Why can she sing and hit all the high notes but my voice can't?

- Who wrote the words to the song?

- Why do Elsa and Anna sing differently from each other?

- Dancing and singing is hard at the same time because I lose my breath; how does that work?

She loved singing because it was fun, but it was also hard to do the type of singing she wanted to do and had a lot of questions. And that's when singing and dancing became more than something "fun to do" and became something she was interested in learning more about.

I learned a very important parenting lesson during this time: My daughter didn't want to hear my answers.

It wasn't that she didn't believe me (or my wife). It was that she wanted to explore these ideas and questions on her own. We had to guide her exploration and give her opportunities to research singing through experiences, not only our thoughts and opinions. The lesson I learned is that *research isn't about reading; it's about learning.*

What did we do? We went to see a Broadway play. Then we went to see a rehearsal session of a high school play. We talked to girls in high school that were singing and preparing to perform on stage. She asked questions. She took mental notes. We watched *The Making of Frozen* video where she could see the people behind the characters practice and record their songs.

We went to a singing lesson. We went to a dance lesson. We went to the ballet (well, my wife did; I didn't). We got "Just Dance" for the Wii so she could practice choreographed dances. We talked to singers at our church. And she practiced to perform at a Christmas service, learning about singing the entire time.

RESEARCH ISN'T ABOUT READING. IT'S ABOUT DISCOVERY.

There was nothing *fancy* about the research we were doing. Instead, we jumped in and tried to learn as much about the subject of singing as we possibly could, through all types of experiences.

And guess what? It was fun! Understanding information through research is a lot of fun for students and adults, as long as we take it on with the right attitude. That's what this phase is all about.

UNDERSTAND
THE PROCESS
OR PROBLEM

PHASE THREE: UNDERSTAND THE INFORMATION

After students have asked a ton of questions, they move into the U of the LAUNCH Cycle. Here, they work to find and understand the answers to all the questions they've asked. They conduct in-depth research in order to gain a deeper understanding of the problem. That understanding will then allow students to navigate the new ideas they generate in the next phase.

Typically, students go back to their massive list of questions and figure out the questions that will lead to specific research. We use the following criteria:

- The questions should connect to the main topic.

- The questions should be specific. In other words, "Why is there suffering in the world?" is a little too broad.

- The questions should be object- and fact-based. So "Why is mauve such an ugly color?" won't work here.

- The questions should ultimately lead to research that will help students find solutions and create products.

This phase can be tricky—especially for elementary and middle school students. When you first introduce the research question criteria to your class, try offering examples and non-examples of inquiry questions. Write the criteria listed above on the board in the form of a checklist. Then have them rate the questions individually, with partners, in a group, and then as a whole class. Next, ask students to work in pairs to create new questions and then use a jigsaw strategy to rate one another's questions. Finally, repeat this process with individual questions. Students should have a solid list of inquiry questions that they will then use in research.

After they have chosen the research questions, consider the types of research in which they might engage. Here are a few common trends in student research with design projects:

- **Problem-Oriented Research:** This research focuses on the causes of the problem and the effects of the problem with solid facts, data, and trends to back up claims.

- **Audience Research:** This research asks questions about their intended audience, including styles, beliefs, values, or demographic data.

- **Market Research:** Like Audience Research, Market Research asks questions about the intended audience but with a greater focus on market forces, including competing works, other solutions that might exist, and behaviors about consumers.

- **Process Research:** This is where students make sense of structures and systems. They focus on how things work and gain the conceptual knowledge they will need to design their final product.

- **Skill-Based Research:** This type of research is common in a design project where students have a specific product in mind. This might be research on the structure of a novel or the techniques used for recording a podcast. It often includes inquiry, research, paraphrasing, and practice.

It is common for people to engage in multiple research styles. For example, an author might ask about process as she works on the structure of a novel. What works? What doesn't work? The same author might engage in audience research before developing a true concept or even market research about what types of books are trending. Or the author might simply look for relevant facts connected to the setting of the book or the main character's career.

Avoiding the Rigid Research Trap

When I (John) first began teaching, I viewed research as something separate from the rest of learning. We did research projects or we kept the research as a phase within a project. It was an end-of-the-year culminating activity. I would spend two weeks walking students through the research process, asking them to take notes on notecards that I had them label according to a rigid system I had developed.

Although I described it as a step-by-step recipe, the truth is it was more like a boot camp for informational reading.

No, you can't ask your own questions.

No, you can't deviate from the topic I chose.

No, you can't ask an adult who might have the answer.

One afternoon, a student called me over with a question. It wasn't about the research topic. It wasn't pertinent to social studies. He wanted to know whether or not whales spoke with dialects.

"Could there be a regional dialect to whale speech?" he asked.

I shrugged.

"We know they have language, but do the words they use vary according to geography? If it did then maybe we would have evidence that language is a product of place."

"Wow," I muttered. "I've never even thought about it."

"Do whales have more than just nouns and verbs? I mean, is there a chance they have syntax?"

"I need you to get back to work," I told him.

His head dropped. He stared down at his shoes.

"I take that back. Why don't you Google it? But promise me you'll get back to your real research later."

"I'll get back to work."

Then it hit me. The phrase "real research" hung in the air, suffocating his curiosity. I turned around and studied the room. Nothing about this felt like real research. See, real research is messy. It's fun. It's a hop-scotch game to and from ideas and concepts and facts. It's an exploration to a distant land. It's a mystery that you're dying to figure out. True research requires structure but only enough to make it work.

I thought about his phrase, "Get back to work." I realized, in that moment, that I had turned an exciting journey into a grueling task. I had transformed an epic experience into a children's version of an expense report. Ugh.

So we scrapped the note cards. We abandoned the specific requirements of how many facts they were supposed to find in a class period. I let them loose to explore on their own. I told them to create their own categories and to find their own sources. Although I kept certain requirements (some sources had to be text based), I allowed them to interview people and access videos or podcasts.

When research is real, it doesn't feel like research. It feels like geeking out. It feels like learning.

Tips for Student-Centered Research

When you're doing research in a design project, you might want to consider the following advice for the exploratory phase:

1. **Make the research process flexible.** I remember giving kids a research grid to complete. Then, I changed it to notecards the next year. Later, I realized that different kids could have their own methods of organizing their research. Some would use a concept map, others would use tables or lists, and still others preferred visual

curation or digital notecards. If your goal is to empower students to be self-directed learners, using a flexible organizational structure is helpful.

2. **Pay attention to bias.** I think educators do a disservice to kids when we teach them that there is a binary difference between fact and opinion when, in fact, it's more of a sliding scale. This hard line robs them of the controversy of "facts" and the conflict they need to experience so they can make sense of their world. This is why we suggest using research as a chance to find and identify bias in sources. Encourage them to pay attention to loaded language and the construction of arguments. Ask hard questions about the omission of certain facts. Examining and weighing out bias takes time (for you and your students), but what they learn makes doing so worth it.

3. **Start early.** Often, research happens at the end of the year. It's sort of a culminating project, often connected to a topic (state reports, animal report, etc.). What if we started research in the beginning of the school year? What if students began seeing research as a normal part of reading and thinking? We've found that Wonder Day projects can be a great introduction to research. On these days dedicated to research, kids take something they are already passionate about and explore it in-depth, then post their findings on their classroom's blog. This guarantees that they have knowledge, while also getting a chance to share their interests and passions with the world.

4. **Expand your definition of sources.** Although students can find information from books and magazines, be sure to encourage them to use social media to connect with experts. When researching social issues, they

can interview people in their community. In the past, I (John) had students conduct Needs Assessments, during which they used polls to collect data and then analyzed the results in their research. For the first time ever, they were able to view data as something deeply human as they researched social issues in their own community. They saw math as inherently social and grounded in a real context.

5. **Provide scaffolding ... but not too much.** Younger kids can navigate research, but it can be tricky. It is often harder for them to find age-appropriate and reading-level-specific sources online. They have less prior knowledge than older students because they've had less schooling and fewer life experiences. Analytical thinking can also be more challenging for younger kids. If you teach elementary students, you may want to provide extra scaffolding for them to work upon. Model the research process, provide sentences stems, and select some of the sources for the students. Keep in mind, however, that there's a danger in taking scaffolding too far and running into the rigid research trap mentioned before. To avoid that trap, start by providing students with basic tools for research and then let them select the help they need when they need it.

We Need a Bigger Definition of Research

The Understanding the Information phase looks different depending upon your specific project. If kids are designing and implementing a service-learning project, they might do needs assessments and evaluate data. If they're researching the setting of their novel, they're probably going to interview a few people and read some articles.

It's for this reason that we need a bigger definition of

research. Research is not limited to a library or a set of books or even a computer. Research is anything we do to answer our questions and make sense of new information. It might involve reading a book, but it might also involve gathering and examining a data set. It can help to think about four key methods of research in which students of all ages can engage.

1: Research Through Reading

The first research approach involves finding information by looking at text-based documents. This is, by far, the most common type of research in school. After all, the information is available at their fingertips. By searching the *interwebz*, they can find the answers and grow in their understanding of the information.

Unfortunately, crap abounds on the Internet. We've had students who were fooled by *Onion* articles. They missed the satirical lens and told me things like, "Peyton Manning is getting a guide dog to go on field with him because he's too old." Um, actually not. We can laugh at comments like this, but the humor abruptly ends when students look up the 9/11 terrorist attacks and begin to believe half-baked conspiracy theories based upon faulty and twisted information.

The truth is that research, especially Internet research, is tricky—for all of us—because anyone can post anything online. This is, again, why it helps to have students engage in research at the start of the school year and practice it continually. As teachers, we can provide supports to walk them through the online research process. Those supports, like the collection and evaluation process listed below, should help them weed out irrelevant and faulty sources.

Practice this research process together. Model the process for your students and then have them do their own research in small groups. When your students are in this phase, it helps to periodically stop and have each person analyze how well he or she is doing at sticking to the steps. In some cases, as you transition to independent research, you may have to pull a small group and work with them. That's okay.

Again, you might need to provide some extra support for younger students. After all, most of the content online is aimed at an older audience. Beyond the concerns about students accessing inappropriate content, the text complexity and reading levels are typically way above what an early elementary student can comprehend. Even when the information is written at a lower reading level, the authors often assume the reader understands certain concepts and ideas that might be developmentally above what a young child can comprehend.

For this reason, you might want to modify the six steps. You can gather five to ten websites and link them to a website of your own. Students can then choose the most relevant sites from what you have curated, then paraphrase the information, and cite the sources on their own. If you want to emulate the search process, you can have each group's sites in one big website (or shared document) and have students search which sites fit their group's topic. Or you could have adult volunteers helping each group in the search process and still use a typical search engine.

Working with a librarian or media specialist can be especially helpful during the research process. By blending together books and online research, they can walk younger students through this process in a way that makes the research come alive. After all, librarians are experts who have studied the best ways to guide students in research. If you have cultivated a good relationship with your school librarian, then this process will work so much more smoothly.

2: Multimedia Research

Some of the best information online isn't text based. Think of the last time you tried to figure out how to learn something new. Chances are you didn't limit yourself to text-based answers. You probably watched a few YouTube tutorials along the way. Sadly, I've seen too many classrooms where students are discouraged from using multimedia resources. They're seen as being less "real" than text-based resources.

Video, pictures, and audio resources make concepts come alive in a way that reading alone does not. It's not that multimedia resources are better, but that they allow students to see things and to hear things that they can't see or hear in a text. It is important to use the collection and evaluation mentioned earlier for all multimedia research. In fact, it can be tougher for students to identify the bias in a video or a picture because there aren't as many loaded words or other language clues. But if a picture is worth a thousand words, then students will face a barrage of thousands of biased words. If students believe that pictures or videos are inherently more accurate (seeing is believing, after all), they may fail to pick up on the bias and indiscriminately accept video or photographic proof.

Collection & Evaluation Process

Step One: Select questions that are fact based and stick to the topic at hand.

Step Two: Use the correct keywords as you begin searching for sites.

Step Three: Decide if the source is relevant.

- Is it on topic?

- Is it from an authoritative source?

- Can it be backed up by other sources?

- Are there any red flags around crazy information that doesn't seem accurate?

Step Four: Analyze the information.

- Is this information accurate?

- Is there any bias you need to look out for?

- Could this be verified by other sources?

Step Five: Paraphrase the information by putting it into your own words.

Step Six: Cite your source.

I (John) noticed this trend when I taught history. I asked students a simple question: "Which is more accurate: words or photographs?" Students overwhelmingly chose photographs. They mentioned how difficult it would be to fake a photograph. However, as we studied "Photoshopped" pictures in their history textbook (a famous Lincoln picture that's actually the body of Henry Clay), the staged photographs, and the bias of angle and composition, suddenly they realized that photographs contain the same types of bias and need to be as carefully evaluated for truth as do texts.

We believe that multimedia is important, if not essential, to phase three of the LAUNCH Cycle. When students learn how to think critically and recognize bias in multimedia sources, they will be able to understand the topic at a deeper level. This knowledge, in turn, helps them in the next phase of navigating ideas and ultimately creating something from scratch.

3: Exploring Data

Another research option involves exploring data. Initially, I wrote the words, "This type of research works better in middle school or high school." But I scrapped that phrase because as I was typing this paragraph, my son called me. He had just arrived home from school and wanted to tell me everything he had learned about sunlight and plants.

"We recorded our data on graphs, dad. And guess what? Even though the plants don't look like they're growing much, I can prove it with my graph!"

When you think of things that typically ignite the passion of a third grader, data and graphing probably don't hit your radar. However, this conversation with my son reminded me that when data is meaningful to the student, it's actually pretty exciting.

Students can explore data in the LAUNCH Cycle in so many different ways. They can go through the search process mentioned in the previous section and focus on published data from public records or journals. If they are doing a design project connected to social issues, they might find statistics connected to the issue they are studying. If their project involves creating a consumer product, they might look at market research connected to certain corporations and sales.

However, they can also record their own data. In his class, my son constantly records data connected to physical phenomena. For example, when his class does a paper airplane launch, he records data about how far the planes fly. He also keeps a record of his plant's weekly growth.

If students are creating a product in your class, they might do customer surveys to get a sense of who would or would not buy a product. They might survey people on specific consumer problems. In the case of a social issue, students might conduct Needs Assessment Surveys to determine perceptions, beliefs, and experiences of the community they serve.

Regardless of the approach, the goal remains the same. Data-based research should always connect to the questions students are asking. When that happens, the data comes alive instead of remaining an abstract set of numbers.

4: Interviews

Interviews are an excellent way for students to understand information. We typically think of research as something static. Students read this or watch that. But when students conduct interviews, they are able to ask questions, get direct answers, and ask follow-up questions. It's a personalized, powerful way for students to learn about a specific topic.

This might involve interviewing a specific person who is an expert on the subject. They might talk to a professor who has taught the subject, an author who has written about it, or someone within a certain profession who has inside knowledge. Other times, they might interview a person who has been impacted by a system, idea, or problem.

Interviews are the hardest type of research to pull off in a class. One option is to encourage students to work through their network outside of school. Parents, family members, and neighbors might help connect them to the types of people they want to interview. Another option is to connect to social media. If you aren't on Twitter, Facebook, and other social networks, we recommend connecting to those communities so you can reach out to a larger network.

Video and audio communication technology makes it easier than ever for students to interview people through digital platforms such as Skype or Google Hangouts. Interviews like this require teachers to be organized and proactive in making sure the equipment is available and connected, and that the interview times are coordinated. That said, setting up a system for interviews is a great job to delegate to parent volunteers.

One of the coolest things we've seen is that adults almost never turn down an interview with a child. When students try to interview someone who might be hard to reach (an industry expert, community leader, or even a celebrity), they often have better success at gaining access than an adult would.

5: Hands-On Research

Research doesn't always *look* like research because not all information can be found in a book, interview, or video. Research about physical phenomena, for example, is often best accomplished with a hands-on, trial-and-error experiment. If a group wants to figure out a new method of transportation, they might want to play around with magnets to see if magnetic trains are actually a realistic solution. Or a group of students working on a video-game project might want to play some video games and take notes on what makes a game addicting.

It's critical that students record what they're learning while doing hands-on research. They might take notes, writing down observations along the way. They might capture what they're seeing in the form of diagrams or sketch-notes. They might record their observations verbally using the voice memo app on their phones.

Regardless of the discovery method your students use, remember that the goal is for them to connect their research to their inquiry questions so they can *understand* the larger problem they are trying to solve. Collecting and evaluating data is important and can even be fun. But the point of the Understand the Information phase is to move students into the next stage of the LAUNCH Cycle.

Visit TheLaunchCycle.com/understand to get more information and resources on Phase 3 of the LAUNCH Cycle. Join the discussion online using the hashtag #launchbook.

CHAPTER 7
NAVIGATING IDEAS

*You have been given the tools you need
to get started. Where it goes is up to you.
The world is your platform.*

– Laura Fleming

Sketches of ideas cover almost every surface of the room. Multicolored webs, bulleted lists, and drawings spill from the whiteboard onto the butcher paper that's been stapled haphazardly to the walls.

Students huddle together in groups, bouncing ideas back and forth, building ideas like sandcastles and then waiting to see if the waves of reality will dissolve what they've imagined.

"What if we tried ..."

"Could we maybe combine ..."

"Wait, wait, wait. If we just ..."

The room looks like a mess. And while the class may seem loud and chaotic, with students moving from place to place, the truth is that this time is highly structured. This free-flowing process and buzz of activity follows a period of quiet and solitude. Through the messiness of this moment, students will transform their ideas into a specific, structured plan that they'll use to build their models.

It's all part of the *Shark Tank*-inspired projects, where students have to develop a product and pitch it as an entrepreneurial idea. Students began by looking, listening, and learning from their audience or potential users. They then asked tons of questions and engaged in discovery methods, including market and process research. Some students gained more understanding through hands-on research, as they played with models of what they ultimately wanted to create. Now, with a clear idea of the problem they want to solve and the audience they want to reach, they are in the fourth phase of the LAUNCH Cycle.

NAVIGATE IDEAS

PHASE FOUR: NAVIGATING IDEAS

Once students have a firm understanding of all the information about the problem they want to solve, they are able to figure out what they want to make. It's tempting in this phase to jump straight into creating stuff, but we recommend that you put on the brakes and have your students create a plan first. True, creating should be messy; and there's a time and a place for making something from scratch. Most of the time, however, when people have created things that truly matter to them, they started with a plan.

Think of it this way: you wouldn't build a house without a blueprint. You wouldn't make a meal from scratch without at least thinking of ingredients ahead of time. And even the glorious mess of a painting often begins with an intentional, deep thought about what the artist wants to compose. There's this natural phase of navigating ideas.

In design thinking, we call this phase *ideating* and in the LAUNCH Cycle, we use the phrase Navigating Ideas. It begins with a process of brainstorming followed by a period of narrowing down the ideas into one specific concept. Afterward, students clarify their ideas even further by creating specific plans.

I (John) was skeptical at first that this ideating phase could work with all grade levels. It wasn't until I worked on a few projects with my own kids at home that I became convinced that even young children can successfully navigate ideas and create a plan. Later, as a technology coach, I found it interesting that primary-grade students could successfully ideate when given a clear picture of the process. Think about how you developed your own plans as a child before creating LEGO buildings or forts or cardboard pinball machines. You might not have called it ideating, but you brainstormed, evaluated your materials and location, and shaped a process or plan before you began building.

Part One: Brainstorming

On the surface, it seems that brainstorming should be easy. We've all experienced meetings when ideas ping-ponged back and forth, and someone frantically scribbled notes and sketched partial concepts on a whiteboard. If you're an introvert who's been part of a brainstorming session like that, you may have sat quietly and watched ideas being volleyed about without ever saying a word. The same thing happens in classrooms. During that high-energy game of idea ping-pong, quiet kids are often left out. As the ideas bounce around, back and forth, introverted students tend to hold their ideas in mental backpacks—and the group never has access to their genius. But that's not the only reason to avoid traditional brainstorming. We found that traditional brainstorming sessions limit creativity in several ways:

- You are more prone to groupthink, whereas members are afraid to share divergent ideas.

- Introverts are less likely to speak up. It isn't simply an issue of being shy. When teachers haven't provided adequate processing time, many students feel overwhelmed by the lack of mental quiet needed to generate new ideas.

- The loudest shouters get the most ideas on the board. Not only that, but marginalized groups are often less likely to speak up in a small-group setting. When their voices are silenced (even if it's unintentional), they are more likely to disengage, and the group misses out on their great ideas.

- The group is likely to place emphasis on quantity of ideas rather than quality. So they end up tossing up more ideas while missing out on some great ideas that need a little time and exploration to hatch.

- It prevents creative risk-taking. If you've ever heard students say, "I don't have any ideas," you can bet that what they really mean is, "I don't know if my ideas are good enough." The truth is that they do have ideas. Great ideas. But they are afraid that their ideas will be ridiculed or ignored. And if students are jumping in and filling the silence, these students don't feel the need to engage in the process.

If old-school brainstorming doesn't work, what does? Well, here are a few ideas:

1. **Have students brainstorm in isolation first.** This allows introverted students to process internally before they enter a group brainstorm. This can be a simple list, T-chart, or idea web. Keep the class absolutely silent, even if kids feel edgy with the silence. Then, move into a pair-share, followed by a group brainstorm.

2. **Have a firm rule that there are no dumb ideas in the brainstorm phase.** Give a silly example if you need to. For example, if they are brainstorming green transportation methods, offer the suggestion of dragons. After all, many dragons are green, right? Mention the

problems with the idea (dragons breathe fire, their
poop is enormous and falls from hundreds of feet in
the air, and they aren't real) and remind students that
the idea still goes on the list.

3. **Experiment with the group structure.** For example,
a round-robin brainstorm might allow all students to
get a chance to share ideas. Here, each student moves
clockwise, one at a time, and shares an idea. Another formatting method might be to have each student
copy and paste the ideas into one shared document,
followed by a period of reading the ideas, and then
adding more thoughts as a group.

4. **Be clear in the specific topic of a brainstorm.** If you
want students to understand the concept of a "total
war" in social studies, a great brainstorm question
might be, "Think of anything, big or small, that you
might need in order to win a war." Emphasize the fact
that random ideas are often some of the best answers
and that there is absolutely no quality control during
the brainstorming phase.

5. **Be intentional about the physical space of a brainstorming session.** You might have a rule that says
devices aren't allowed. You might make sure that all
students are in a circle around a table. In some cases,
you might want to model the body language of listening and participating. Some of the best brainstorming
happens when students can stand near the whiteboard
holding their lists of ideas and adding ideas one at a
time to the board.

6. **Create breaks for individual reflection.** If you start
with an individual brainstorm and you move to a
group brainstorm time, end the session by having

students look at the group's list and adding at least three personal new ideas based upon what others have written. You might want to ask, "How can you build on another person's idea?" or "What is something you might be missing?"

7. **Have a brainstorm leader whose job it is to write down the ideas and guide the brainstorm.** This person's job is to make sure no one is criticizing an idea and to also focus on making sure the brainstorm isn't sticking to one train of thought for too long. Coach the student leader to use the sentence stem, "How about ..." or "Have you considered ..." to help the group move on.

8. **Move students around.** We don't do this all the time, but to avoid groupthink, we occasionally ask students to rotate to other groups so they can add or hear a new perspective.

9. **Try multiple visual methods.** We love lists as brainstorm tools. That said, sometimes a web works better because it gives students a visual framework for adding onto the ideas that are already there. We believe the best web creation tool is a giant piece of butcher paper and markers. Yes, computers are awesome; we love technology. But markers are pretty great, too. And there's just something about writing in vibrant colors that helps ideas flow.

10. **Don't use a timer.** Experience has taught us that timers make kids risk averse. They end up panicking and failing to think as creatively as they might have without the pressure of the clock. Our suggestion: let brainstorm sessions end naturally.

Our Brainstorming Process

In our classes, students begin brainstorming by working alone. This allows each student to have a specific voice in the brainstorming process. Some students write their ideas out in lists. Others choose a web or combine images and words in a sketch-note style of brainstorming. The students choose the format individually.

Next, we move into small groups. At first, students simply write out all their ideas in the form of a list. In some cases, students might share a Google Doc and add their text simultaneously. In other cases, students might take turns round-robin-style and add an idea to a list on a piece of paper. It is critical that all students are sharing their ideas and that nobody makes any comments, negative or positive, about the quality of ideas. Typically, a group will look over the list and add details that they hadn't considered before seeing others' ideas.

Once the list is generated, the groups turn their ideas into webs. This allows students to make connections between thoughts and potentially consolidate similar concepts. This is when the room's energy (and volume) jumps up a few notches. Also during this time, students leave their original group to move to other groups (thus adding fresh ideas to the mix). We usually assign a number to each group member and say things like, "I need all threes to find another group. See if there are any ideas that they are missing." This creates the right kind of disruption that often leads to more innovative ideas.

Next, students return to their groups. When they do, we encourage them to add some "bad ideas" to the list. While that may sound odd, we want students to see that some of the best ideas have come from bad ideas. We also want them to offer up radically different ideas. Additionally, this request for bad ideas frees risk-averse students to share thoughts, even if they aren't confident about them. If someone shares a really bad idea, it's fine. In fact, it's great. This the bad-idea phase, after all!

Finally, students combine ideas that seem totally unrelated. A documentary about immigrants and a podcast about economics might become a media package blending together a documentary, podcast, and blogs about the economic forces that influence immigration.

While this process may seem complex, it works at all grade levels. In fact, young students are often better at flexible thinking than older students. They can combine two genuinely different ideas and come up with something better. As with earlier stages of the LAUNCH Cycle, you might want to add some supports to make this process easier for younger students. For example, you might model the process as a whole group. You might offer a graphic organizer when doing a web. You might skip the part about the "bad ideas" and jump straight into combining two ideas. The key is to do what works best for your students.

BRAIN BOOST
THE POWER OF DIVERGENT THINKING

The best brainstorming happens when students engage in divergent thinking. Divergent thinking is a process of seeing multiple options and viewing solutions in a different way. Divergent thinking is what happens when you find connections between things that initially seem disconnected. It's also what happens when you find unconventional uses for a specific item.

Divergent Thinking and Innovation Go Together

In a culture that encourages sameness, divergent thinking is a break from the norm and may challenge students who want to please you by giving the "right" answers or ideas. So how do you get them to think beyond the obvious? We like Pixar's approach. When navigating ideas for their stories, Pixar's creative team is intentional about considering divergent ideas. In fact, rule nine in their "Rules for Storytelling[1]" states, "When you're stuck, make a list of what *wouldn't* happen next. More often than not, the material to get you unstuck will show up."

Notice that we put structures into place to promote divergent thinking during the brainstorming process. The first is the chance to combine two seemingly unrelated ideas. When students do this, they often find a solution that they wouldn't have previously considered. The second is when they create a list of solutions they wouldn't want to choose (borrowing from the Pixar model). Often, this leads them to reconsider their own blindness. Finally, the use of webs in brainstorming allows students to make important connections between seemingly unrelated concepts.

PART TWO: CHOOSING AN IDEA

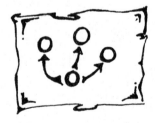

This is the part where students start evaluating which ideas would work best and why. If part one was all about getting great ideas out, then part two is all about narrowing those ideas down. And if you're doing it right, expect there to be plenty of debate and discussion.

Step One: Adding Details

First, you'll want to have students focus on finding any missing details—ideas that aren't on the brainstorm list or web. This step allows students to look for gaping holes in their potential design ideas. The following questions can help guide students in this step:

- What are you missing?

- Is there an idea that makes you think of a slightly similar idea?

- Are there any details you could add to an idea so that it makes more sense?

Step Two: Consolidating Ideas

Here students identify ideas that can be grouped together. Ask students to create categories and add ideas to the categories. Then they can draw a circle around ideas they really like. Or they might write a new idea and scratch out two or three related ideas. The following questions can help guide students in this step:

- What trends do you see?

- Are there any ideas that could be combined?

- Which ideas are the most similar?

Step Three: Setting Up Criteria

Students establish the criteria for what makes each of their ideas work. It's important here that students focus on the positives. They will have the chance to look at the drawbacks of ideas later. However, in this step, they are focused on the potential of each idea. Setting up the criteria doesn't have to be anything fancy; students don't need to create a formal rubric.

When you encourage students to answer a few questions like those that follow, they will naturally sort out what works.

- What are you looking for in a design?

- What do we want it to accomplish?

- What are the criteria for a great idea?

- What features do you want in your design (originality, realism, feasibility, time constraints, material constraints, knowledge of how to make it, etc.)?

Step Four: Narrow Down the Best Ideas

Here, students look at the general set of ideas and narrow it down to their top two or three. In some cases, they might combine ideas again (similar to step three), and that's okay. These processes are supposed to be flexible.

- Which ideas are the most original? Are there any ideas that have already been done well by someone else?

- Which ideas seem the most realistic?

- Which ideas could we actually accomplish with our time constraints and our materials?

Step Five: Choose the Idea

Here's where the process tends to get the most contentious. If students are truly stuck on their final idea, they might want to play a game of rock-paper-scissors for the ultimate decision. Better yet, they might want to create a separate pros-and-cons chart or even assign a score for their criteria and then rate their top ideas as a result.

- Which idea seems to solve the problem the best? Why is that?

- What are the pros and cons of each idea?

- Which one will ultimately lead to the best success?

- Which idea fits with the skills of our group?

BEFORE MAKING ANYTHING, MAKE SURE YOU HAVE THE PARTS

PRODUCT IDEA

AUDIENCE

ROLE

TASKS

SOLUTION

PART THREE: FIGURING OUT THE PARTS

After figuring out a general idea for a design, students begin creating a plan for their product. We use the following acronym to help students figure out their plan:

Product Idea: a clear idea of what your product will be, how it will work, and what materials you will need

Audience: a specific audience who will consume/experience the product

Role: your team has specific roles in creating this product

Tasks: a specific timeframe in which to complete the project

Solution: a rationale explaining what problem your design solves and why it will work

Before your students make anything, make sure they have all of the PARTS.

Product Idea

Students start out by creating a product sketch. The focus of the sketch is to show how the product works. As students work on their sketches, it's helpful to remind them that the goal is expressing the functionality of their product. The sketch doesn't have to look pretty. What you want is a sketch of what they are going to create. If the product is three-dimensional, they could sketch it out from different angles. If the product is a service, they might want to create a flowchart. If they are creating a novel or a magazine, they could sketch out potential layouts, character sketches, plot diagrams, or storyboards.

We use the following criteria when explaining what a great product sketch includes:

- A visual element that makes it easy to see what the product will be

- A clear title and subtitle that offer a short explanation of what the product will be

- Plenty of annotations that explain exactly how things will work

- Arrows, lines, or other markings that allow the reader to see what is going on

- Any types of symbols or visuals that will help people understand conceptually how their product will work

After sketching their ideas, students create a product description. This description should answer the following questions:

- What is your product?

- How does it work?

- What is it made out of?

The description doesn't need to be complicated. A simple paragraph is often enough.

Audience

In most cases, your students will have identified a general audience in the first or second phase of the LAUNCH Cycle. However, it will be helpful to them to clarify the specific traits or demographics of their audience before they proceed to the Creating Phase. The following questions can help guide the process:

- Who is the intended audience?

- What are some ways you will reach this audience?

- Who is *not* your audience?

- Why will this product help your audience?

Roles

Here's where you have students look at the larger tasks listed in step three and develop specific group roles. Here are some guiding questions:

- What are the different roles necessary for completing this project?

- How are the group roles being decided?

- How will your group members communicate with one another?

- What are some of the tasks that each group role will need to accomplish?

Your students may need your help in developing specific group roles for the project. Particularly if you're working with younger students, you may want to identify the roles and tasks and allow your students to focus on who would be the best choice for specific roles.

Tasks

After thinking through the product, audience, and roles, students move deeper into planning. Here, they are actually beginning the process of project management by creating a general timeline for their product.

- When is it due?

- What are the stages?

- What are some of the big tasks that need to be accomplished?

Next, they break it down into tasks and sub-tasks. The following chart can be helpful for identifying the project's needs. Note that under Necessary Materials, the specific item listed might be something that another group member will create.

Date	Larger Task	Sub-Tasks / Steps	Responsible Member	Necessary Materials

BRAIN BOOST
THE BIOGRAPHY OF AN IDEA

In his dissertation, "Reframing Creativity as the Biography of an Idea: Developing Learning Narratives that Describe Creativity as a Distributed and Participatory Process[2]," Clapp writes:

> *Fostering creativity through education has long been a priority. Despite this imperative, many educators and policymakers retain traditional, individual-based understandings of creativity that are both out of sync with contemporary systems-based creativity theory and incongruous with the increasing emphasis on group invention and geographically distributed teams seen in business, education, and government.*

Clapp's study examines three core questions:

1. What are the observable ways individuals participate in and contribute to the ongoing development of group-generated creative ideas?

2. What types of individual and group learning take place during the development of group-generated creative ideas?

3. How does what individuals and groups learn throughout the process of developing group-generated creative ideas inform and influence the evolution of the ideas being developed?

> *By chronicling the unfolding histories—or "biographies"—of creative ideas, I track the evolutionary arcs of "Reverse Outlet" and "Static Fashion," two group-generated ideas. The histories of these ideas serve as learning narratives that describe the various ways in which individuals participate in the development of creative ideas—and the learning that accrues to those individuals along the way.*

So what does this mean for our students?

Forming a list of required materials should happen during the *Tasks* part of planning. The following are some of the guiding questions you might want to use:

- What are the materials you need?

- What materials do you need that you don't have? Is there a way to get those? Are there substitute materials you can use?

- Where will you store your materials?

- Who will bring specific materials?

Solution

In the final section of the PARTS planning, students should write a rationale explaining what problem their design solves and why it will work. Doing so forces students to clarify the specific problem in a way that makes sense. Sometimes this clarification leads to a creative breakthrough, and they modify their initial product plan and change up their tasks. Most of the time, though, they have a specific problem in mind, and they are able to articulate a rationale for why their product is the ultimate solution. The following questions can help along the way:

- What are the problems that this product solves?

- Why will this product solve the problem?

- What will you say to people who ask, "Why should I consider this product?"

- How is your solution different from what is currently out there?

THE BIOGRAPHY OF AN IDEA

Edward Clapp works for Harvard's Graduate School of Education and is a Project Director at Project Zero. He holds a doctorate of education and masters of education from Harvard, a masters of letters in poetry from the University of Glasgow/ Strathclyde, and a bachelor of fine arts in painting from the Rhode Island School of Design. In addition to his academic pursuits, Edward's poetry and fiction works have been published in national and international literary magazines, and his plays have been produced in New York.

Why do I include this long line of credentials? Because they intimidated me. I (A.J.) was so nervous when I first met Edward that I wondered, *What do I have to share with this guy that is of any importance?* And at the same time I thought, *How can I pick his brain?*

Contrary to my preconceptions that he would be hard to talk to, I was relieved when Clapp turned out to be one of the nicest and most down-to-earth individuals I had ever met. And he lived up to my expectations in terms of picking his brain. As we talked about creativity, he brought up an interesting point.

"What if instead of telling the biographies of individuals who are widely seen as creative geniuses, we tell the biography of the ideas that they are most known for? For example, what if instead of telling the biography of Albert Einstein, we told the biography of the Special Theory of Relativity? We would tell the biography of that idea, highlighting all the different players who have historically participated in the development of that idea, the different roles those individuals have played, and the different twists and turns that idea has taken as it has wended its way in the world."

I stopped and thought for a moment. He was right. We tend to celebrate individuals for their creative genius instead of looking at how an idea grew and changed and morphed into something bigger than originally planned.

Facebook began as an idea to get back at a girl. Apple started out as a side project to make some quick cash. Virgin Airlines began after a flight was canceled and Richard Branson wanted to see a girl.

When we think of these companies and individuals today, we tend to link the idea directly to the person and shout about their creative genius. But in doing so (as Clapp pointed out), we fail to recognize the collaborative effort and input from many other individuals who have worked to make the idea a success.

Clapp's research is simple, but clear. Reframing creativity as the biography of an idea allows for more people to navigate ideas and join the collaborative process. Then, not only are our students working on these ideas together, but they are also finding a sense of accomplishment from the collective creations that they put out into the world.

Think back to the PARTS Framework:

Product Idea: a clear idea of what your product will be, how it will work, and what materials you will need

Audience: a specific audience who will consume or experience the product

Role: your team has specific roles in creating this product

Tasks: a specific timeframe in which to complete the project

Solution: a rationale explaining what problem your design solves and why it will work

The roles become much more intriguing for students when *every* role in the creative process has purpose and meaning. Reframing the solution as a collective effort of navigating ideas together empowers all students involved to find success.

WHEN STUDENTS NAVIGATE IDEAS TOGETHER

Not long ago, I (A.J.) spent some time working with teachers at Gideon Hausner Jewish Day School in Palo Alto, California. The topic of discussion was how to take Project-Based Learning (PBL) to the next level so that their students could do more collaborative, authentic work (instead of only some of the time).

As we talked, one group of elementary teachers explained that they wanted to shift from small-group projects and participate in a massive, whole-group endeavor that included every subject area. Later, as we brainstormed ideas on how to do this, I asked, "What was the moment last year when your students felt most accomplished?"

Several immediately responded, "Last year's play."

After navigating numerous ideas together and with students, they combined a few concepts and determined to put on a play around a specific time period in history. The language arts and social studies teachers helped the students write an original script and screenplay. The math and science teachers empowered students to create STEM-based projects like special effects and building the set and backdrops. Everyone in the grade level was involved in turning this idea into a reality.

The teachers told me it took a lot more time than they originally had planned, but the experience and results were worth it. The students turned the idea into an epic event when they decided to put on a live play for all the parents and students from the other grade levels.

This *biography of an idea* came to life as every student played a role in pulling off the major live event. A reporter from the local newspaper came out to take pictures and write about the collective effort. The students proudly shared about the experience of working with their teachers and with other students to make the idea a success—together.

When students and teachers collaborate to navigate ideas, the product (or play) becomes much more than one person's accomplishment. This *togetherness* takes group work to a new level; and when an idea is successful, the experience is meaningful to everyone involved.

Visit TheLaunchCycle.com/navigate to get more information and resources on Phase 4 of the LAUNCH Cycle. Join the discussion online using the hashtag #launchbook.

Notes

1. David Price, "Pixar Story Rules (One Version)," *Pixar Touch Book*, May 16, 2011, pixartouchbook.com/blog/2011/5/15/pixar-story-rules-one-version.html.
2. Edward Clapp, "Reframing Creativity as the Biography of an Idea: Developing Learning Narratives that Describe Creativity as a Distributed and Participatory Process," Harvard University, Graduate School of Education. 2014.

CHAPTER 8
CREATING

The classroom should reflect the world for which we are preparing our students. If we are asking them to create, innovate, and be outstanding as graduates, then our classrooms should be creative, innovative, and outstanding places to learn.

– Jenny Magiera
Author of *Courageous Adventures*

Houston, we have a problem.

Sitting at a massive technology conference listening to a keynote about creativity, I (John) cringed as the speaker showed slides that paired inspirational quotes alongside images of nature. *Click.* An image of a kid blowing on a dandelion and watching the seeds float away into the sunset. *Click.* A scene of a man relaxing against a rock, looking out at a sunrise. *Click.* The message: Creativity is a natural thing and we simply need to let it happen.

As I sat there, I couldn't help but think that the speaker's definition of creativity was incomplete. Don't get me wrong, dandelions are awesome. I have been known to stop mid-run just to take a few seconds to blow on dandelions and watch the seeds fly around (only to realize, later, that I need to take allergy medicine). The scenes were inspirational, but not one of the images showed someone *making* anything.

The truth is that creative work is, well, work. For all the talk of creativity in schools, one of the reasons so few people engage in creative work is that it's really, really hard. It's easy to plan. It's easy to dream up ideas. It's easy to be the dude staring blankly at a sunrise. It's so much more challenging to be the one bent over a workbench trying to figure out how to solve a complex problem.

There is no shortcut to creative work. When you really care about a project, you will pour your entire being into what you make. You will expend massive mental, emotional, and even physical energy, knowing all along that failure is a distinct possibility. Your product might not turn out the way you had imagined. Your audience might not like it. Or worse, they might ignore it.

And there's no blueprint for your product because you are creating it as you go. The more innovative your idea is, the less certain you will feel about its success. Even when you have a solid plan (as is the case with design thinking), the moment you start creating, you run into challenges. Huge challenges.

Yes, creative work might well be the most difficult thing you'll ever do.

So here's the deal. Creativity is not easy. It's not fast. It's not perfect. It's emotionally draining. It requires hard work and patience. So why do it? The simple answer? We are human. We've always been creative. We are natural makers. And when we create, we come alive. Ultimately, this feeling of energy and engagement leads to better learning.

If you assign a project and get back thirty of the exact same thing, that's not a project. That's a recipe.
–Chris Lehmann,
Principal of Science Leadership Academy

CREATE A PROTOTYPE

PHASE FIVE: CREATING

After navigating ideas, students move into the creating phase. This is the part that kids tend to love—at first. It's hands-on. It's multi-sensory. It is what we imagine when we think about creative work. At times, students get lost in their work. With a clear sense of context based upon their research and a clear plan before them, they may even enter a place of *flow* in which they focus so intently on the creative process that they lose sight of everything else.

In these moments, making feels like magic.

On the other hand, this can also be a phase where students hit "project fatigue." Sometimes they simply can't figure out how to finish a particular part of their design. The problems can feel too insurmountable. The vision of what they will create doesn't square with their actual skills. Certain students get distracted and zone out. Others get frustrated and want to give up entirely. Often, the group dynamics fall apart over creative differences (not unlike a rock band). Tempers flare and students walk away in tears, saying, "I just can't do it."

It's important to remember that these moments are not moments of failure but rather a normal part of the LAUNCH Cycle. Think back to the Apollo 13 story. The astronauts and engineers had spent years planning for the launch. They had built a core team inspired by the vision of another flight to the moon. Despite all of that planning, they hit that gut-wrenching moment and said the famous words, "Houston, we have a problem."

Ultimately, their ingenuity and innovation pulled them through a terrifying moment of crisis. No longer was their creative work about designing rockets and planning missions (the fun part of the process), but about surviving an immense challenge.

The truth is, you will have at least one "Houston, we have a problem" moment in the midst of a design project. You might be tempted to call it a failure or to believe you are somehow doing it wrong. But here's the thing: These moments are a chance for your entire class to work together to solve a major problem. And while these situations can feel stressful (an understatement), these very moments will define you as a creative teacher and foster the kind of innovation and imagination you hope to see in your students.

EVERY ROADBLOCK IS A CHANCE TO SOLVE A PROBLEM.

As you prepare to bring out the creativity of your students, be aware of the potential challenges both you and they will face. We've outlined a few here and provided some strategies you can use to tackle them.

Challenge #1: It Takes Time

Creative work often starts out slow, messy, and inherently frustrating. Fear, even reticence, is not uncommon. You don't want to screw up. You are constantly monitoring and adjusting. You have no sense of workflow. You stumble around. You take too many breaks. You give up too easily, only to turn around and stubbornly stick with something that will never work out.

Over time, though, you get faster. You don't need to monitor and adjust quite so often. You reflect while working rather than waiting until after the project is complete (or completely abandoned). You learn the skills and mental habits you need— the ones that initially tripped you up in your creative journey. Then one day, you realize, "I'm actually pretty fast at this."

The same thing happens with students. Creative fluency simply takes time to master. For all the talk of life, productivity, and growth hacks these days, creativity isn't something that can be hacked. The creator simply has to persist through this phase—one messy, slow step at a time. It can be frustrating, but it is vital for growth.

So when kids are doing video editing for the first time, it will feel like it takes ages to get one fifteen-second clip created. When they write their first blog post, the learning curve might feel intense. When they design a bridge, their first few attempts are likely to crumble.

Speed isn't a bad thing. After all, watch a five-star chef and you'll see that speed matters. Watch a master teacher and you might realize that she knows how to plan an entire unit quickly, making split-second decisions that seem to come out of nowhere. See a muralist at work, and it might look frantic (even if it is calm and mindful). But what you miss in watching these experts is the learning process.

You didn't witness the hours that the chef spent awkwardly chopping carrots or the slow and clunky brush strokes the muralist used before ever getting the permission to paint an entire wall. And do you remember how long it took to write a lesson plan when you were a pre-service teacher?

If we want students to hit a place of creative flow, we need to give them time to experience this phase. We must allow them to be excruciatingly slow. There's no shortcut. They can't bypass the necessary learning and discovery, trial and error. They simply need more time to work through it.

The first strategy is to allot plenty of time. And believe us—we get that, given the breakneck pace of school, this notion of deliberately embracing huge, inefficient blocks of time is a foreign idea. Maybe it's time we slowed down a little.

In addition to the gift of time, there are a few other ways you can help them manage the challenges they face during the creating stage. For example, by providing templates that students can modify, tutorials they can access, and one-on-one targeted help when they need it, you can encourage and equip them to try again. Sometimes it's hard to know whether you should let a student struggle or step in and provide guidance. How do you know when to provide an example and when an example might actually stifle creativity (as students copy too many ideas from the example)?

Challenge #2: It Feels Scary

I'm (John) writing a novel. That is to say, I'm working on writing a novel. And it is work. Even though I have no deadlines for this particular project and no one is breathing down my neck, I'm frustrated. The story isn't working. The characters are too flat and the plot is too formulaic. I haven't built in enough suspense. I've gone through the LAUN phases of the LAUNCH Cycle, but I just didn't anticipate some of the issues I'm facing.

What makes this process even more frustrating is that writing is something I love doing, and I'm good at it. And still, day after day, I sit down at my computer and clench my fist. Stuck.

I would love to say that the problem is external, that some outside person is getting in the way of my creative work. I'd love to say I just don't have enough time to get things done or that I'm too distracted. However, that's not the case. The truth is, I'm afraid.

It's when I feel afraid that I am most tempted to give up. Maybe you can relate.

The fear isn't a product of frustration or difficulty. It stems from the thoughts running wild in my mind. I'm afraid that the plot won't play out. I'm afraid I will waste a few days and have nothing to show for it.

I know, I know. Mistakes are a part of learning. Revision is necessary. Things take time to evolve. And yet, in the midst of creating, fear creeps in.

Often, for students, it is fear that kills creativity. Frustration is a part of the learning process. It isn't fun, but it's necessary, even beneficial, when you learn to persist. In contrast, fear is the force that pushes us away from creative risks by saying, "You'll never figure this out. You're wasting your time." It's what happens when a student says, "I'll never learn to code," or "I'm just not a good writer," or "I'm really not an artist."

So many people in our world give up entirely on creative work because of fear. We quit dancing because we are afraid of looking stupid. We quit singing because, one day, a single off-key note convinced us that we couldn't sing. We quit *stopping and observing and wondering* because we are afraid of being unproductive.

And so the world has all of these adults who were born creative and yet, somewhere along the line, they quit making stuff. They let this beautiful part of themselves die because they were afraid. It's a tragic, wasteful loss.

What do you do to mitigate these fears for your students so they don't give up?

1. **Share your own fear as a maker.** I believe that teachers should have their own Genius Hours, so they can experience the fear that happens in the midst of making. I actually think there is a value in being creative (especially in a new realm) around students. Last year, I worked next door to an art teacher who painted while her students painted. It was a strategic move. She wanted her students to see her make mistakes and get frustrated, so they would know that even veteran artists get frustrated.

2. **Promote a growth mindset with students.** When students are focused on growth, we see a change in their expectations and mindset toward learning. Instead of trying to prove how smart they are, students instead work hard to become better.

3. **Encourage risk-taking as a part of your classroom culture.** Take risks as a teacher. Try new lessons and strategies and tell students, "I'm experimenting with this." Act goofy. Be silly. Draw doodles on the board, even if you aren't particularly artistic. Take those risks and don't be self-deprecating. Don't mock your own work. Simply say, "I'm still learning." Ultimately, your modeling of risk-taking leads to a classroom culture of creative risks.

4. **Switch to standards-based grading.** Students become risk averse when they are worried about grades. The traditional system of averaging grades (and placing completion above mastery) ultimately means students are less likely to take creative risks. However, when they know they can revise their work and ultimately create something worth putting in a portfolio, they see mistakes and revision as a natural part of the creative process.

5. **Keep the creative work meaningful to students.** Part of the reason I refuse to give up on my novel is that I love what I'm doing. I am making something that matters to me. So both the product and the process are something I love (even when I'm frustrated). If that passion is not present in your students' projects, it's pretty hard to keep them intrinsically motivated.

6. **Ultimately, fear festers when it's hidden.** It's that monster that's only terrifying when it's dark. But take it out in the open, bring it out into the light, and things change. When you create classroom culture that values vulnerability, where kids can be open about their fear of creative failure, then fear becomes less terrifying.

Challenge #3: Classroom Management Issues

Chaos is inherent to the making process. Things can get noisy, not to mention messy. Emotions can run high, and kids can get frustrated. While we want students to embrace the mess of making, we also want the class to be safe. We want materials put away in the right places. We want the noise level to allow for group collaboration and communication.

For this reason, it helps to develop a classroom-management plan for prototyping. Admittedly, crafting a strategy like this can seem complex, but we promise that having a clear set of expectations will help you minimize discipline problems and maximize innovation in your classroom.

Reflective Questions for Creative Learning Spaces

The following are a few logistical things you might want to consider in the prototyping phase:

- What behavioral issues might arise? How will you prevent these?

- What procedures and expectations will you need to teach ahead of time? Consider:

  » How will students get materials?

  » How will you handle noise?

  » How will you handle movement?

  » Are groups allowed to talk to one another? If so, what does that process look like?

  » How will you handle students finishing at different rates?

  » What kinds of "brain breaks" will you offer to students who need to walk away from the prototype?

  » What materials will you use? Where will you store these materials? Where will students put their prototypes when they leave the class period (or move on to a new subject)?

- How will your role change? How will you spend your time when students are in the prototyping phase?

- Are you comfortable having administrators and other leaders walking into your classroom during the prototyping phase? What kinds of concerns might outside teachers have about your class's creation process?

Challenge #4: Not Enough Resources

I (John) used to feel like my students weren't doing "real" prototyping because we didn't have the same amount of materials as other classrooms. We never had 3-D printers. We never had power tools. Then, I saw *Caine's Arcade*, the story I mentioned in Chapter 3, and I started thinking about my own kids and the crazy worlds they created with the leftover boxes after

Christmas. I thought about the cardboard pinball machine we built the day after Christmas when my kids ended up neglecting all of their own toys in order to play with what they made. I thought about the pillow forts we built. I realized that prototyping isn't about perfect realism.

It's about imagination. It's about dreaming. It's about making things with your own hands, even if what you are making begins with nothing more than scraps of cardboard and a roll of duct tape.

Forty-Five-Minute Design Challenges

Usually, I like to give students ample time to create. But during the year I taught sixth grade ELL, I implemented shorter design challenges. That year, I had the same group of students all day in a class that, by law, had to be hyper-structured (we had a four-hour block of reading, writing, oral language, and grammar). On Tuesday, we didn't have an elective class, so I had forty-five bonus minutes to plan something entirely different.

Initially, I planned a Genius Hour project. However, after two weeks, it wasn't working. I realized that Genius Hour actually required more structure and time than I had considered (which is why I ultimately restructured my oral-language hour to be Genius Hour).

I considered making this short forty-five minute block a silent reading time or beefing up our math block. Instead, I landed on an UnGenius Hour. Taking to heart the truth that limitations can (sometimes) actually boost creativity, my students had limited time, limited resources, and limited options—and they loved this time. Sure, it sounds counterintuitive, but these limitations actually created a certain level of freedom that pushed kids to think divergently.

Students arrived to their groups after lunch and found a box with a few supplies and a short design challenge. The instructions might be, "Design a board game that isn't boring," or "Build a bridge." Other times, it was simpler: "Make something."

During the next forty-five minutes, students built a prototype. It took a few weeks before the first group realized they could use the box itself. It took another week or two for students to realize they could do quick research on the Internet and plow through the design cycle we had been using with our other design projects.

Sometimes their creations bombed. Sometimes kids got frustrated when things didn't work. But that was okay. Mistakes were allowed. Nothing was graded. It was simply forty-five minutes of planning, making, testing, and revising.

What's interesting is that students never once complained about the limitations. Nobody ever said, "I can't be creative unless I have the right resources." No one ever said, "I can't get this done with those oppressive time deadlines you are putting on me." Instead, the limitations became a source of their creative thinking.

I used to think creativity was all about thinking outside the box, and sometimes it is. Sometimes, though, it's more about re-purposing the box. Sometimes it isn't a blank canvas or a crisp white page. Sometimes it starts with a limited timeframe and a limited set of resources. In these moments, the lack of options actually pushes people into thinking more creatively.

Challenge #5: It Gets Boring

"You okay?" I (John) asked the student who was staring at the wall. He was supposed to be working on building a video game.

"Yeah, Mr. Spencer. I don't feel like fixing the scripts," he said.

"The nice thing about coding is that it's not dependent on how you feel. So why don't you get to work?"

He turned around and glanced at his computer. Slowly, he plugged away. The work was a grind at first, but ten minutes later, he got into it. I realize that my words to him might have seemed dismissive of his feelings. However, there is an aspect of creative work that requires us to be dismissive of our feelings. I used to believe that creativity would always lead to fun. I thought that if I crafted the right project and included a high level of creativity, students would enjoy every lesson. I was crushed, then, when I saw students getting bored.

At first, I thought there was something wrong with the lessons. However, over time, I started to realize that any creative work has an ebb and flow of excitement and boredom. A chef faces tedium in prep work. A painter has to deal with minute details. A mechanic often tries tons of diagnostic tests before finding a solution.

It's hard, as a teacher, to step back and allow students to endure that tedium. We want kids to be happy and enjoy learning. In these moments, it's tempting to tell students to just move on and let it go. Skipping the boring parts seems easier than encouraging them to push through and get stuff done.

A deeply held cultural belief tells us we have to be inspired to do creative work. You wake up and feel like painting, and then you frantically paint on a canvas for as long as that euphoria lasts. You hit a moment of brilliant inspiration, and then you pen a song. But that's not actually how creativity works.

If you look at the habits of highly creative people, you'll see that they share these four traits:

1. They make mistakes. Loads of them. Their work sucks at the beginning, just like yours and just like mine.

2. They poop. I like to remember that everybody poops because it's sort of a disarming fact. The greatest creative geniuses are still absolutely normal. They eat and drink. They stub their toes and yell out expletives. They fall in love.

3. They get scared that no one will like their stuff. They get frustrated when stuff doesn't work. They get bored with the tedium of what they're doing. But still . . .

4. They make stuff.

That last one is critical. Really. The only reason someone is "highly creative" is that they make a ton of stuff. How'd that writer get so good? Well, she wrote. A lot. She sat down and wrote a ton of words and the combination of consistency and focus made her prolific.

Ultimately, when you look at people who are highly creative, you see that they are actually pretty different from one another. Some work early in the morning, others late at night. Some work in a crowded cafe and the noise soothes them. Others work on a mountaintop where they can clear their minds. Others stick to a tiny windowless office. Some prefer to work in a scattered mess and others prefer a clean, minimal workspace.

But the common trait for all creative people is work. They all work on their craft. Every. Day. And they spend hours and hours doing it. You can't productivity-hack your way through it. You just have to spend hours working at your craft until the stuff you make goes from kind-of sucky to okay to prolific.

What does this mean for teachers? How do we help students get past the boredom and hit a place of creative flow?

1. **Treat boredom as a choice.** A few years back, my family visited a lake, but we left all of our supplies at home. We didn't have any toys or any swimsuits. Initially, our kids complained about boredom, but when we reminded them that boredom is a choice, things changed. They skipped rocks. They explored the trail near the lake. Eventually we invented a game that we played with an empty water bottle. Students need to know that they can control their decision to be bored.

The goal isn't to occupy yourself with devices and keep yourself distracted. The goal is to say, "Here are my limitations. Now what can I do that is fun, meaningful, or challenging?"

2. **Learn to distinguish between boredom and confusion.** Here's where you can use breaks strategically. Sometimes what feels like boredom is actually a mental block. Sometimes all a student needs to do is take a walk and come back to the work.

3. **Keep working, no matter how you feel.** Knowing that you can continue to work even when you feel uninspired liberates you from your feelings.

4. **Remember what's important.** Certain creative tasks are boring. They just are. You can't necessarily spice them up. However, when students remember that these tasks are connected to something that matters to them, they are able to finish them and move on.

5. **Cultivate creative habits rather than simply winging it.** Creative fluency takes time to master. Cultivating the right habits and showing up day after day will help you find your creative flow.

We are human. We've always been creative. We are natural makers. And when we create, we come alive.

Brain Boost
Sometimes Boredom Makes You More Creative

Have you ever found yourself having amazing creative break-throughs while you're on an airplane? Initially, you feel bored (even though you're in a metal container that's hurtling through the air at mind-blowing speeds), but after a period of time, you hit a creative breakthrough. This is similar to those amazing ideas you have when you take a shower or when you're stuck in traffic.

Surprisingly, some of the best creative breakthroughs happen during moments of boredom. Part of this is due to the relaxed nature of boredom.

Boredom also sparks creative thinking because when we are truly bored, we will search for new ways to do things. Karen Gasper and Brianna Middlewood, researchers at Penn State University, demonstrated this idea by having study[1] participants watch videos that would elicit different emotions (including boredom), and then asking them to complete a remote-associates test. This test asked participants to look at three unrelated words and make a connection to a fourth item.

In another study, Sandi Mann and Rebekah Cadman, researchers at University of Central Lancashire, asked a group of participants to copy names from a phone book[2]. Next, they engaged in a divergent-thinking activity where they had to find multiple uses for a cup. The participants who were the most bored by the phone-book exercise ended up doing the best on the creative exercises afterward.

Challenge #6: It Doesn't Have Meaning

When I ran a 20% Time project in my classroom, a few things were immediately apparent to me:

1. My students had a hard time unleashing their own creativity in a school setting.

2. I had a difficult time helping them find their passion to create.

3. Almost all of the successful projects had a driving purpose behind them.

The past few years, as I've helped other teachers establish inquiry-based projects like 20% Time and Genius Hour in their classrooms, I am always asking students what their purpose is in whatever they are working on. I explain that I ask myself this same question when I'm working on something creative. And the answer can't be grades (for students) or money (for teachers). How often is the only "purpose" for learning tied to grades? How often is the only "purpose" for work tied to money? What happens to learners who don't care about grades, and workers who want more purpose in their job than just a paycheck? Chances are they stall out, fail to move forward, and move on to something else. If we want creative students, we'll have to allow them to choose a purpose for much of their learning. If we want creative teachers and leaders, we need to allow for purposes other than financial compensation.

Their purpose could be to change the world, or make a video game that 1,000 people play, or start a band. As long as they truly care about that purpose, they'll have the dedication needed to keep going when the process is difficult.

So how do you find your purpose? Start by sifting through the noise and all your interests. Use the following strategies to uncover what matters most to you and to your students.

1. Take notice of what you do when no one is "telling you what to do."

This is a big one. What types of activities do you do when you are not working, learning, or being told what to do? To dig even deeper, ask yourself these questions:

- What do I do on weekend mornings?

- What do I do after dinner during the weekday?

- What do I do when I have time off from work or school?

- What do I do when I'm sick and at home?

- What do I do late at night and early in the morning?

When you analyze your answers, chances are, many of the activities you list will be consumption (watching TV, playing a video game, using an app, reading a book/magazine/blog) or they'll be communication (hanging out with friends, talking with friends, chatting online, etc.).

If there is anything you do during these times that is considered "creating" or "making," be sure to star that on your list. Maybe it is writing, or working on your car, or putting together a stereo system, or making up steps to a dance, or writing song lyrics, or doing a craft (digital or not). We'll revisit these activities later.

2. Take notice of what you do when you are "supposed to be doing something else."

It's easy to get off task. One minute you're working on a project, and the next you've shifted gears and your project gets left behind. So where does your attention go? What types of activities do you veer toward—at work, school, or at home—even when you are "supposed to be doing something else"?

We all have responsibilities and priorities. We have things we "need to get done." However, when we put those responsibilities or priorities to the side in order to work on something else, that is a telling sign of our passions. Make a list of the activities you're drawn to and separate them based on consumption, communication, and creating/making activities.

3. What types of information do you read and watch?

Maybe all you read is sports magazines and all you watch is ESPN. Perhaps all you read is fashion blogs, and all you watch is *Project Runway* reruns. Or maybe you read and watch a variety of things. That's fine. Regardless, make a list of the kinds of information that appeal to you.

We consume what we are interested in, but often it is a way to relax. Now think about what types of information that you consume to get pumped up and ready to go! Those need to be starred on your list as well.

4. Create your own "March Madness Interests" bracket.

It may sound silly, but we like the March Madness bracket better than a Venn Diagram (ugh). Download a blank March Madness bracket from TheLaunchCycle.com, and fill it with the interests you listed in the previous questions.

Creativity is as much an attitude as it is an action. It is a decision to persist, to show up and do the work, even when you don't feel like it.

Do you have sixty-four interests?

Now, eliminate interests based on what you would like to spend time doing if you won the lottery and could do anything. This is a fun way to force yourself to make some tough decisions about where to put your time, energy, and focus.

5. Give yourself a trial period.

You've narrowed down your interests into viable passions. However, it may still be difficult to pin down which interests are actually your true passions. So give yourself a trial period. Take each of your "Final Four" interests and passions and spend as much time as you can working and creating with that passion for a week.

During this trial period, note which of your creative passions puts you into a state of flow where you lose all sense of time because you are so focused on the task at hand. If you want to know which passion to pursue, follow the one that leads you into flow.

6. Get started!

This is where your creativity begins to have purpose. Passion is what gets you going. It's what fires you up about a new project or opportunity. It may lead you to shout your excitement from the mountain tops. But purpose keeps you going when your enthusiasm fades. Purpose is not the feeling, but the *why* that comes from your passion. Why you are passionate is the ultimate driving purpose. Purpose drives your everyday actions because there is a reason behind everything you do. When you have both passion and purpose, you're on the path to creating something awesome.

Remember…

Creativity is as much an attitude as it is an action. It is a decision to persist, to show up and do the work, even when you don't feel like it. The creative process cannot be forced, and it cannot be faked. It must contain purpose or it will never be finished.

Visit TheLaunchCycle.com/create to get more information and resources on Phase 5 of the LAUNCH Cycle. Join the discussion online using the hashtag #launchbook.

Notes

1. Karen Gasper, Brianna L. Middlewood, "Approaching Novel Thoughts: Understanding Why Elation and Boredom Promote Associative Thought More Than Distress and Relaxation," *Journal of Experimental Social Psychology* (Elsevier), May 2014.
2. Sandi Mann, Rebekah Cadman, "Does Being Bored Make Us More Creative?" *Creativity Research Journal*, Vol 26, Iss. 2, 2014.

CHAPTER 9
HIGHLIGHT AND IMPROVE THE PRODUCT

*Failure is an option here. If things are not failing,
you are not innovating enough.*

- Elon Musk
Founder of SpaceX and Tesla

My (John) son decided he wanted to make something similar to a Rube Goldberg machine. We put together PVC pipe, bricks, and anything else we could find to create a path that would guide a metal ball from our roof to a tiny bucket on the ground. On the surface, this seemed like an easy enough creation to make. But getting the ball to land in the bucket proved to be far trickier than we'd anticipated. Even the slightest movement of the pipes caused the ball to stall or drop to the ground—not into the bucket.

So we tried.

We tried again.

We tried ten more times.

Then another ten times.

We tried until he was nearly in tears, staring at the ball, stuck in the middle of one of the pipes. It seemed as if, instead of making progress, we were regressing. After going back inside and getting a drink of water, we tried ten more times. Then another ten times.

We spent ninety minutes making tiny, mind-numbing modifications. A few times, he threw his hands up in the air, tears welling up in his eyes, and said, "It's not going to work." Then, after wiping his eyes with his shirt sleeve, he went back to work and tried again. He stood back and glared at the contraption. Arms folded and scowling, he shook his head. Suddenly, he snapped his fingers and adjusted the top pipe.

He climbed up the ladder and dropped the ball in the container. It trailed down the roof, twirled around a pipe, jumped another pipe, hit a brick, popped up, landed in another pipe, swirled slowly down to a table, pinged up and down against some more bricks, until it found a groove in the table that it traveled down and, joy of joys, fell into the tiny bucket on the ground.

"It worked!" he screamed, jumping up and slamming my hand in a high five. "I can't believe it! I can't believe it! It really worked!"

That evening, I thought about the contrast between the project my son had created and his experience at school. At home, he was able to move incrementally toward his goal. He had the absolute permission to make mistakes. No threat of a bad grade overshadowed him. No rigid curriculum maps or deadlines held him to a schedule. We had all the time in the world for him to make tiny adjustments until he finished the task.

In design thinking, we want kids to embrace mistakes as part of the learning process. Kids begin the project knowing they won't get it right on the first try. That would actually be boring, like jumping to the top level on the first turn of a video game.

When kids do design projects, they understand that each mistake is a chance to figure out what works and what doesn't work. When students have the permission to make mistakes, they define success as growth and learning. They recognize that failure isn't really failure at all. Ultimately, they become less risk averse. They try new things ... even if it means trying seventy-seven times before reaching the desired outcome.

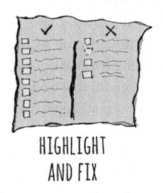

HIGHLIGHT AND FIX

PHASE SIX: HIGHLIGHTING AND IMPROVING

In the LAUNCH Cycle, students immediately move from creating their products into a revision process that includes highlighting what's working and not working and then fixing the problem. In the traditional design cycle, this Highlighting and Improving phase is called a "test" that is followed by reflection or empathy. However, we believe that this phase goes beyond simply testing a prototype. The goal here is an ongoing mini-cycle of highlighting the strengths and weaknesses of the product and then improving it based upon that feedback.

We prefer to use the word *improve* rather than *fix,* because fix implies something is broken. However, *improve* tells students that what they created is good and they have the chance to make it even better. It's a subtle distinction, but a powerful one.

Students begin this phase by examining the criteria for analyzing their work. In many classes (especially with younger students), the criteria has already been set by the teacher or, better yet, through a conversation between the teacher and the students. Next, they highlight the strengths and the weaknesses of their product. Then, based upon the feedback that they gather through both others' and their own evaluations and observations, they improve their product. They continue this mini-cycle of Highlighting and Improving until they are ready to launch their product to an audience.

As teachers, we have always struggled with this phase. Looking back at our design projects, we realize how many times we've truncated this cycle. We get impatient with projects that drag on and are eager to move on to the next project. Unfortunately, that means our students may have missed out on making something amazing.

However, in those situations when we built in ample time and provided the appropriate structures for the Highlighting and Improving cycle, students learned more from the process and had a product that they were truly able to launch.

This Takes Courage

The Highlighting and Improving phase can feel scary for students. They don't want their product to fail. No one does. For all the talk about embracing failure, the truth is that failure sucks. No author says, "Man, I hope this piece I've written ends up being scrapped completely from the book." No coder says, "I really hope this string of code ends up failing to work." Failing isn't fun. It's infuriating. At times, it feels devastating. Think of the last time one of your lessons tanked. Chances are you didn't leave the lesson smiling and saying, "I'm so glad I made all of those mistakes."

Students are no different from adults. They don't want to feel as if they wasted their time on something that didn't work in the end. It can feel terrifying to look at their work honestly and say, "How did this turn out?" And the more time, energy, and effort they put into their product, the more emotionally charged this phase feels.

But here's the thing: As much as we naturally hate mistakes, each mistake is actually a step toward the final product. In creative design, each new product sample is called an iteration. In technology, we talk about a product being "in beta." When we look at design this way, revision becomes an opportunity rather than a liability. Critical feedback becomes just that: critical. And critical isn't bad. It's crucial. It's vital.

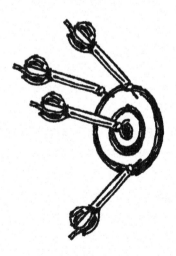

It's a myth that great products are created by geniuses who get it right the first time. In reality, we stumble our way into greatness. We "mistake our way" into genius. Design, creation, and innovation don't happen on a clearly marked path. They are the stepping stones on an epic journey. At times, you will be convinced that you are lost and will never make it to the end. As with the Creating phase, there are no hacks, no ways to bypass the revision phase. Only through constant feedback, retracing your steps, and laying new stones will you find your way and reach your destination.

Embrace the journey! You may just discover a destination that's better than you'd imagined. Regardless of the outcome, the journey offers you and your students the chance to grow into courageous heroes. Yes, this phase is terrifying. But when you create a safe place for your students to face their fears, you're allowing them the opportunity to develop something much more valuable and lasting than a simple product: character.

The Power of Pivoting

Remember that bizarre cartoon about a man who gets a book about monsters and as he deals with his fears the monsters disappear? Or what about that strange animated movie about the dog that runs into a zombie and aliens? If you've never seen these films, there's a good reason. You don't work for Pixar or Disney animation. However, they were early versions of the classic *Monsters, Inc.* and the mess of a first version of *Bolt*.

Both movies evolved over time through a series of iterations. That's Pixar's model. They take years to develop a movie through storyboarding, building, analyzing, and improving. When you hear phrases like "success, no matter what" and "everything it takes," you likely think of high-stakes environments. Tons of pressure. Super-tight deadlines. But that isn't the case at Pixar where "whatever it takes" means literally doing whatever it takes—and often that requires more time and freedom.

One of the hallmark processes Pixar's creation teams use is called the Brain Trust. Here, they emphasize the role of candor in highlighting what's working and what needs to be improved. These meetings are safe, open environments where anyone in the room can offer honest feedback. The Brain Trust process empowers the writers and digital animators to solve problems, find innovative workarounds, and get out of the tunnel vision that can happen within a creative team.

This feedback allows Pixar to pivot in the midst of a project. By constantly analyzing their work, team members are able to create small, incremental iterations. That freedom to change also allows the company to be more nimble—unencumbered by rigid ideas and deadlines. It seems counterintuitive that this additional time and emphasis on revision would make the company as a whole more efficient and effective. But that's precisely what happens. Pixar continually produces some of the most creative cinema of our time.

This culture of revision is at the heart of the Pixar story. It began as a technology company. Its leaders repeatedly experimented and failed. Steve Jobs had to bail them out on several occasions. In this early phase, the company pivoted like crazy. But through this process of making things and testing them out, Pixar's creators eventually found their identity as master storytellers. All the mistakes they made were a part of the journey. They were a part of the discovery process.

Scott Adams, the innovative creator of *Dilbert*, once said, "Creativity is allowing yourself to make mistakes. Art is knowing which ones to keep." The idea here is that mistakes are simply failed experiments. And sometimes those failed experiments are actually the very things that lead to innovation.

Highlighting the Strengths and Weaknesses

Students can more easily highlight the strengths and weaknesses of their product when they have a clear idea of what they are looking for. The following are a few examples of what students might use:

- A rubric with specific descriptions (such as a writing rubric)

- A pros/cons chart

- A split A/B where students can compare two specific ideas or applications

- A set of exemplars that students can compare to their own work

- A checklist of features

- A list of criteria to test (such as the weight a bridge can withstand)

- A set of thoughtful questions for reflection

After setting up the criteria, students highlight the product's strengths and weaknesses. In some cases, they will test to see if something works. For example, if your students built a model bridge, they will test it by adding weight. Other times, they need qualitative feedback. If your kids are making a documentary, they might watch a segment of it and jot down notes about what is working or not working. Or they might simply list little mistakes that need to be fixed and then make a list of strengths to build on.

Older students might want to break up feedback into categories, like form, functionality, style, etc. Doing so can help them distinguish between critical elements to test (does this work?) versus smaller details (how does this look right now?). For example, in a narrative, the structure and style of a story should be tested and revised first, before moving into the fine-tune-editing stage.

With younger students, it helps to provide a simple list or rubric that they can use to analyze their work. You can use the sentence stem, "Does this have a _____?" or a set of directions, such as, "Look at the _____. What are some good things about it? What are some things that could make it better?"

Students should have a list of smaller action items that they can then work through to improve their products. Some students can keep this list mentally. Others need to write down a checklist. Either way, students go back to their product and make improvements.

There's no perfect approach to the Highlighting and Improving cycle. If you like for your students to be on the same page the entire time, you might want to block off certain class periods for analyzing work and other periods for improving their products. If you prefer the workshop model, you'll probably want to let students decide when they want to highlight their work and when they want to improve it.

We have found that it helps to keep the cycle short so students can make improvements faster while breaking up the monotony that sometimes goes with revising one's work.

The 20-Minute Peer Feedback Process

Groupthink is a danger for any team. After brainstorming and working together on a project, it's easy to develop a group mindset. This is a negative byproduct of a very positive, collaborative vision and creation. So how do we shake things up and help groups avoid tunnel vision?

One option is through a 20-Minute Peer Feedback process. The way this works is simple. Members from different groups pair up and engage in a five-step process. Each part takes two minutes. You, as a teacher, can keep a timer going and prompt with "next" when it is time to move to the next phase.

In the first round, the first partner gives an "elevator pitch" sharing the product so far. They might have a physical model or a fragment of the writing. The goal, though, is to keep it short. Next, the second partner asks clarifying questions while the first partner answers the questions. The rule is that there cannot be any feedback given. It has to be question and answer.

Afterward, they move into the feedback stage, where the second partner gives specific feedback. This is followed by paraphrasing. Finally, they land on next steps. When this is done, the partners switch roles and repeat the process for round two so that everyone has the opportunity to receive peer feedback.

Peer-Feedback Phases

Time	Phase	Description	Partner A:	Partner B:
0-2	Elevator Pitch	Partner A explains the process, product, or idea in two minutes	Explain your process, product or idea	Take notes on what you are hearing or listen actively
2-4	Clarifying Questions	Partner B asks clarifying questions without giving any feedback	Answer clarifying questions	Ask clarifying questions
4-6	Feedback	Partner B gives feedback to Partner A	Take notes on specific feedback you have gotten	Offer feedback in the form of two things that worked well and one idea for an improvement
6-8	Paraphrase	Partner A paraphrases what he or she has heard from Partner B	Paraphrase what you have heard	Listen to see if the paraphrased information is correct
8-10	Next Steps	Partner A makes a list of future revisions	Make a list of future revisions	Check the list of revisions

Swap places and repeat!

Making Revision Engaging

Traditionally, revision is designed from a deficit mindset. In other words, students only see it as something that is broken—as a sort of debt they have to pay to get the work up to par. A student turns in an assignment and a teacher tears it apart with the dreaded red pen. The student then looks at all the criticism and fixes it in order to bring it back up to the right standard.

In this model, the revision process is almost entirely teacher-initiated. Students rarely get the chance to reflect on their own work and figure out what they need to fix. Usually, the revision process is hurried and has to stick within a tight time deadline. The grading system puts a premium on getting things right the first time, so even if a student resubmits the work, the result is an average of the two grades. This style of revision punishes mistakes rather than treating them as a natural part of the journey. All of this creates a sense of anxiety with revision.

It's time to think differently about revision. Revision is a chance to *refine* what we've done. It's not only about fixing what is broken but continuing to tweak the great thing we already made. Improving, revising, and reworking result in the many iterations that students make as they progress through the journey.

There are certain things you can do to keep the testing and revision stage interesting for you and your students. Here are a few suggestions from John:

1. **Change up the grouping.** A fresh set of eyes brings a new perspective in the testing phase. I love the writer's workshop model for that reason. But I wonder if that should be happening more in a math or science class, too.

2. **Help students become better critics.** What if we had a sort of peer review process that went deeper than "two things I like and one thing to change"? Thoughtful,

constructive criticism takes time, but it's why creativity ultimately requires thoughtful consuming.

3. **Emphasize that all great products went through many iterations before they worked well.** Share your stories of testing and revising. Let students see the revision phase is meant to be a positive experience. It's the chance to tweak things and make them more awesomely awesome.

4. **Break it up.** Allow students to test a particular part of their prototype and revise it before moving on to another area of testing and revision. Sometimes a big testing phase (here's everything wrong with your video) can feel overwhelming. We'll get into the testing-revision mini-cycle here soon.

5. **Create the right atmosphere for revision.** Deep revision requires a thoughtful intensity that's borne out of silence. Finding that silence can be tricky in the chaos of a maker project. We've found that it helps to provide quiet spaces for revision—even if that space is down the hallway. Ideally, we would like to have more spaces for quiet thought throughout school.

6. **Devote more time to revision.** Part of why so many students struggle with the revision phase is that the deadlines are too tight, or all revisions are expected to be done at home.

7. **Use student conferencing.** I've used two types of conferencing in the past (and we'll discuss this more in the next chapter). The first was consulting (where the teacher provides advice when students felt stuck) and the second was coaching (where the teacher led students through self-reflection).

The Highlighting and Improving phase is never going to be entirely easy. Revision will always carry an element of fear and have boredom built into it. With practice, it can get easier and begin to feel like a normal, natural part of the design process.

PIVOTING KEEPS YOU OPEN, FLEXIBLE, AND WILLING TO ADAPT.

How One School Highlights at Every Grade Level

"Inquiry. Impact. Innovation."

Stunned, I repeated my question to Bo Adams, chief innovation officer at Mount Vernon Presbyterian School.

"Bo, can you tell me again what your focus is for student learning at Mount Vernon?"

He chuckled, "Well, that's it. Inquiry. Impact. Innovation. That is our focus every day here at Mount Vernon."

I went a bit deeper with the next question, still surprised by the simplicity of his answer.

"What is your vision or mission at Mount Vernon?"

Again, he recited, from the top of his head, the school's vision for learning:

"We are a school of inquiry, innovation, and impact. Grounded in Christian values, we prepare all students to be college-ready, globally competitive, engaged citizen leaders."

Wow. I had to take a moment to collect my thoughts. This was a school that not only had a vision and mission they believed in, but they were also living it out in every classroom.

Bo Adams, who also heads up the Mount Vernon Institute for Innovation (MVIFI), showed how their school was highlighting and improving upon student-centered learning at all levels. When elementary students at Mount Vernon saw that their trash cans were filled with recyclable materials, they began asking questions:

- *Why is no one recycling?*

- *Is it that they don't care, they don't know, or they forget?*

- *How can we increase recycling, especially in the cafeteria?*

These questions led to some research. These students asked classmates about recycling. They talked to teachers about the school recycling program. They analyzed the placement and color of recycling bins in the cafeteria.

They came to the understanding that most teachers and students knew they should be recycling, but it was hard to remember to do it in the middle of a rushed hurry to leave the cafeteria. So the students brainstormed ideas for making it easier to recycle and then navigated the possible solutions together.

Finally, the students decided to gamify the recycling process. They added a cardboard scoreboard and completely changed the way students recycled in their school. Now students were rewarded for recycling, and the gamification led to a higher level of recycling than ever before. As Bo told me the story, I couldn't help but ask if this was the work of a teacher or the students. Bo let me know that this was student-centered learning at its finest. Sure, the conditions were created by the teacher, but the learning and research and creating was done by all the students.

This wasn't the only time Mount Vernon students created and highlighted their work. In partnership with an enrichment organization called Break Into Business, Mount Vernon's fifth-grade classes spent months developing business and entrepreneurship skills. Students created sixteen small businesses and eventually went before a *Shark Tank*-style panel of judges at a local theatre before they set out to pitch their products at the Chick-fil-A home office.

As written about in a local paper[1]:

In order to be well prepared to launch their small business at the Chick-fil-A home office, the students have been following along with the three Ps of entrepreneurship—product, price, and promotion. They first brainstormed an amazing product idea and tested it through market research. The teams next developed a detailed budget of expected revenue and expenses. Finally, they launched extensive promotional campaigns by creating business websites, T-shirts with their logo printed on the front, posters, slogans, and more.

Given the hard work and creativity that these students have demonstrated thus far, there is no doubt the students are ready to LAUNCH! The students have elected to donate at least 10 percent of profits to Lighthouse Family Retreat, then they will split the remainder. To highlight the work these students did, they went a step further. They wrote about their experience in the Entrepreneur Magazine blog for the entire world to see!

This type of creative work is also happening at the high school. The Mount Vernon Presbyterian School hosted a symposium in October 2013 that brought faculty, students, civic leaders, and business entrepreneurs together to discuss innovation. The gathering engendered considerable conversation, but the discussion that made the strongest impression on students was how they could apply concepts of innovation and change to their school.

"They asked, 'If school is meant to prepare people for real life, then why doesn't school *look* like real life?'" said Bo Adams, the school's chief of learning and innovation. "Out of that, they conceived ideas to bridge real-life and school issues."

IF SCHOOL IS MEANT TO PREPARE PEOPLE FOR REAL LIFE, THEN WHY DOESN'T SCHOOL LOOK LIKE REAL LIFE?

BO ADAMS

Those questions sparked a new concept at the Sandy Springs school, and after a few months of planning, the Innovation Diploma was launched. The degree allows students to get practical experience at tackling real-world problems with the support of faculty and outside mentors. The program accepted applications, and of the twenty-two students who interviewed for spaces, twelve were accepted to start the course the following school year.

The first real-world learning included spending time working alongside the Center for Disease Control (CDC). The CDC even invited the students to their headquarters to speak about their work. Instead of consuming and listening, students were actively creating, proposing solutions, and collaborating with the CDC.

Often when we look at creativity in a school setting we see it being limited by space, time, and resources. What the stories from Mount Vernon show us is that we are usually more limited by our views regarding what students can accomplish and how they can impact the world.

As much as we want students to highlight what works, we also need to be right by their side, supporting, promoting, and highlighting their work in multiple ways and formats. Bo Adams sums up this need perfectly: "For so long, much of the conversation in education has been primarily about 'teaching.' Let's change the paradigm and make LEARNING the primary focus of our conversations."

Visit TheLaunchCycle.com/highlight to get more information and resources on Phase 6 of the LAUNCH Cycle. Join the discussion online using the hashtag #launchbook.

Notes

1. http://www.chick-fil-afoundation.org/our-blog/helping-atlantas-youth-break-business

CHAPTER 10
IT'S TIME TO LAUNCH

The currency of the future is ideas.
- Sabba Quidwai

On July 20, 1969, millions around the world gathered in front of fuzzy television sets to watch the impossible. People had followed events closely in the newspaper, listened to reporters talked about it on the radio, and watched updates on the nightly news. Finally, it was here. It was happening. It was a moment so incredible that even now there are conspiracy theorists who can't accept that it actually happened.

IMAGINE IF NO ONE HAD SEEN THIS.

Just eight years prior, President John F. Kennedy had offered a bold idea. "I believe that this nation should commit itself to achieving the goal, before this decade is out, of landing a man on the moon and returning him safely to the Earth."

Now, the world watched in eager anticipation as a shuttle approached the moon—this mysterious object that, just centuries before, had been an enigma to humanity. And now we were approaching the furthest boundaries of human imagination.

Families gathered around in disbelief with the words, "The eagle has landed."

They watched as thirty-eight-year-old Armstrong scaled the ladder and stepped foot on the moon. Then, with the first steps, Neil Armstrong spoke the iconic words, "That's one small step for (a) man and one giant leap for mankind."

Amid a brutal Cold War and a divisive world, that moment was one of the highest moments of the twentieth century. But what if it hadn't been? Imagine the same moment without an audience. Imagine the astronauts launching the rocket, landing on the moon, and collecting data in isolation. Perhaps they would have sent the information to a tight-knit community of "real scientists" and avoided sharing it with the public. They would not have had to deal with the distractions of the television cameras. Buzz Aldrin could have snapped the same pictures of Earth and kept them in a scrapbook.

What would we have missed if that NASA mission had remained a quiet, private affair? See, landing on the moon wasn't explicitly practical. It didn't solve a pressing problem of the time. However, it inspired millions of children to dream and explore and believe. Suddenly, astronauts were heroes to emulate. And kids believed they could do anything, dream anything, and be anything, through ingenuity and perseverance.

The Apollo 11 moon landing reminds us of the power of an audience. The feat would have been just as magnificent had they accomplished it in secret. However, when shared with the world, it became a part of our public consciousness. It inspired innovation, exploration, and creativity for generations to come.

LAUNCH TO AN AUDIENCE

THE FINAL PHASE

In the traditional design-cycle model, people move from testing what they've created all the way back into the first stage to start over on a new problem. In our opinion, that model leaves out a seventh phase. We call it Time to Launch! Does it need an exclamation mark? Yes. Yes, it does. We believe that this missing stage is one of the most powerful aspects of design thinking.

This is the phase where students send what they've created to an authentic audience. However, great products do not end up in the hands of the intended audience on their own. Whether it's a social solution, an innovative idea, a work of art, or a tangible product, these great, creative ideas have to be "sold" in order to reach the right people.

For this reason, we view launching as a distinct stage—and one that is bigger than simply publishing or finishing or presenting your work to the classroom. It's the idea of building up a launch strategy and sending the product to the right people by using methods of persuasion.

Ultimately, this phase leads to more awareness. When the product reaches the intended audience, you and your students will have the chance to pay attention to user feedback and ultimately ask more inquiry questions, conduct more research, and work on ideation and prototyping. The cycle continues.

Misunderstanding Marketing

If this final phase sounds like marketing, it's because it is. We believe students need to learn the art of marketing. Initially, I (John) had a hard time with this term. I wanted to call it something different. As an author and an artist, I viewed marketing as trickery, and I didn't want to be a part of it at all. I thought "selling" somehow devalued the creative work.

That misconception couldn't have been further from the truth. If students are designing something for an authentic audience, don't we want them to get it into the hands of that audience? If that's the case, shouldn't students learn the best strategies they can use to reach that audience?

The common, deep hatred of selling most often stems from fear, especially for creative types. We're afraid that it will look like selling out. We're afraid that it will look disingenuous, that somehow it will strip the virtue out of what we created. Our culture tells us that creative work should be done for the sake of creative work. And sometimes that's true. Sometimes. There's a time and a place for journaling or writing a story for a small group for an intimate poetry slam. However, there's also a place for going big. If you created something you are proud of, why not send it to the world?

When you've created something that solves a problem for another group of people, then promoting it is actually an act of service. Think of it this way: in the business world, the best salespeople don't have to convince you to buy the product. Instead, they have to believe in the product and find the people who will believe in it as well. They're like matchmakers for problems and solutions.

In addition to looking like a sellout, another fear often stands between the creator and the launch: rejection. On the whole, people are afraid of rejection. When you make something and you send it to a small group, you are hedging your bets. You can aim low, reach the goal, and move on. You never have to hope for anything bigger. And the inherent risk in hope—real hope, gritty hope—is that you'll be disappointed. So you keep the audience small because you don't want to be crushed by the failure to reach a larger audience.

Sometimes the fear is more internal. I tell myself, "I don't want to impose. I don't want to annoy others." But if I'm honest with myself, I am insecure about my creative work. I'm not entirely sure that it's good enough for the whole world to buy into. And instead of selling, I politely mention it at the margins of a conversation. I suggest it subtly. But I avoid marketing.

Here's the thing, though: if you spent days working on something, then the universe deserves it. If you made something and you poured your heart into it, chances are it is awesome. And if it is awesome, the world needs it. We need more awesome in our world. When you market something you made, you are adding awesome to the universe. You're not imposing. You're not being annoying. You're adding awesome to the universe.

Not everyone is going to get your idea, product, or service. In fact, most people aren't going to like what you have to offer at first. That's okay. Chances are, what you created appeals to a specific audience. In business, this is called product-market fit. The key here is to know that it's not personal if people don't get it. Some people like pumpkin-spice lattes. I don't get it. I never will. However, there are hordes of people in America who embrace all things pumpkin related. My distaste for pumpkin-spice lattes has nothing to do with the barista behind the counter. That flavor is just not my thing.

My point is that we need to separate ourselves from the product and understand that when we launch and market, we aren't saying, "You need to buy this." What we are saying is, "Here's why this might be right for you," and then letting the audience figure out if it's a good fit. This isn't easy. It requires a certain level of courage that can be hard to muster. But if you have an idea, a product, a service, or an event that you care about, you ultimately want it to reach an audience. That process of reaching out to the right people is the heart of marketing. And we're convinced that this is a valuable skill that kids need to learn.

When we include marketing and launching into the product-design process, we send students the message that their work matters. We are saying, "The world needs to see this." Moreover, we are encouraging courage and risk-taking. We are telling them, "The world needs more awesome, and what you made is going to make that possible."

In most cases, the "sell" part is a little easier for a classroom. After all, most student design projects are usually free. However, the same fear and insecurity you might feel in doing creative work is often not only present with students but also amplified. Many students are scared that their work isn't good enough for the world. They're convinced that it's not worth sharing. They're terrified of rejection. But if they don't launch their work to the world, the universe misses out on your students' dose of awesome.

Seven Reasons Why Kids Should Learn Marketing

Marketing isn't typically something students learn in school. It's generally reserved for college courses or, perhaps, briefly mentioned in a senior economics class. But just because they aren't learning it in school doesn't mean students aren't familiar with it. After all, we live in a world inundated with marketing. Our students are a part of a consumer culture. When they learn about marketing from the marketer's perspective, they grow as critical consumers while learning what it means to share their work with an authentic audience. With that in mind, we have created a list of reasons why students should learn marketing:

1. **Marketing is a vital life skill.** The notion of a product-market fit, the functions of delivery systems, and the art of persuasion are not simply business concepts. These are used in social services, in government agencies, in helping professions, and in fine arts. Although the term has an economic connotation, the truth is that we are marketing constantly in life.

2. **Children need an ethical foundation to marketing.** Take a glance at the news and you'll see horrible stories of trickery and manipulation in the name of marketing. These stories point to the need for children to develop a set of marketing ethics. When they learn appropriate and honest strategies in design projects, they learn firsthand why successful marketing doesn't have to involve manipulating people.

3. **Students learn about rejection.** The hardest part of marketing is the potential rejection you might face. This is why, as teachers, we're often tempted to shield students from the pain they might experience. However, when they learn that the vast majority of the world will reject their creative work, they gain insight to how creativity actually works, and they realize that

a product-market fit often includes boatloads of rejection. However, in the process, they also experience authentic success when their work reaches an audience.

4. **Students develop courage.** Marketing is one of the riskiest aspects of creative work. It is terrifying to say to the world, "This is what I made, and this is why you might like it." It can feel arrogant. Kids might feel like phonies. The rejection mentioned in the last point leads to very visceral fear. That's why most people never market. However, when students learn how to market at a younger age, they grow courageous.

5. **Students grow in their creative confidence.** For all the rejection kids may face, they will also experience success. People will, at some point, love what they made. This leads to creative confidence. Sure, we are supposed to be internally driven. We aren't supposed to need external validation. However, kids are dying for true affirmation, and when marketing works well, it ultimately affirms their skills, personality, and ideas. This, in turn, leads to an affirmation of their identity.

6. **Students become critical consumers of information.** When students learn about ethical marketing, they also learn about the unethical, manipulative tactics of certain corporations. As they learn, they gain a more critical understanding of how they (and others) consume information.

7. **Students become more empathetic.** Marketing is ultimately about getting a product into the hands of the right people. In order to do this successfully, students need to develop a strong sense of empathy with their audience.

What Launching Looks Like for Students

Students have typically defined the intended audience in the first and second stages of the design cycle. In some cases, they have refined the intended audience in the ideation and planning phase. Often, they have refined their concept of the intended audience through the ideation and prototyping phases. So they should have a clear picture in their minds regarding who will ultimately receive the product.

But how do they get it to the audience? How do they get the audience to buy into it? Whether it's a tangible product, a creative work, an event, or a service, students will want to send their finished work to an authentic audience. In this phase, students can think about the logistics of how to get the audience to see the product (awareness) and receive it (buy it, consume it, use it).

Part One: Clarifying Your Audience

In this phase, students spend time rethinking and clarifying their intended audience. While they should have a clear audience in mind from the beginning of the LAUNCH Cycle, sometimes in the process of prototyping and editing, students discover that the audience is different than anticipated. As they gain new clarity about their true audience, they can shift their focus to a new audience or pivot to a similar audience.

Even if the audience remains the same, students might need to refine their concept of the audience and perhaps even learn more about its preferences, behaviors, and beliefs. The following guiding questions can be helpful:

- Who is your audience?

- Where do they meet regularly?

- What beliefs, values, or attitudes do they have?

Part Two: Figuring Out Your Methods

Once students have figured out their intended audience, they will need to think through how exactly to reach it. One potential strategy for older students is to teach them about basic marketing techniques like framing, lead magnets, and funnels. For younger students, it might make more sense to think about broader ideas like whether or not you want your launch to be online, in person, or both.

- How will you reach your audience?

- What mechanisms will you have that will allow your audience to share information about your product with others?

- What systems or strategies will you use to reach your audience?

- What platforms will you use?

Part Three: Convincing People to Buy In

This is the part that typically feels the most normal to students. They live in a consumer world where they are bombarded with targeted advertisements. If anything, it might be helpful to guide them through advertisement criticism and set parameters for what types of techniques are deceptive and unethical.

In this phase, students might create a logo or a set of graphic designs. They might develop a short advertisement or a viral video. They might work their networks to push word-of-mouth conversations.

The following questions might help during this part:

- How will you make your product stand out?

- What methods will you use to convince your audience to buy / consume / use / receive your product?

- What marketing techniques will you use?

- How will you persuade your audience without being deceptive?

- What marketing ethics will you set for yourself?

Part Four: Launching

Finally, your students are officially ready to launch! Here's where they create a plan to build up hype for the official launch. If they have an event attached to their project, this is their chance to build up anticipation by getting commitments and RSVPs. If the launch is online, this is their chance to set up a countdown before the launch so that it doesn't come out of nowhere.

- How will you release your product?

- What trends are you seeing as you launch it?

- What kind of lead-up did you use to build up to the launch?

- Will your launch be in person, online, or both?

- What will you do to build up anticipation before the launch?

We need more awesome in our world. When you market something you made, you are adding awesome to the universe.

The Power of Launching

In ninth grade, I (A.J.) cut my thumb on a saw in wood shop and had to get stitches. It wasn't too bad, but that was the last year I took "shop" class in high school. I had enjoyed making our CO_2 cars in middle school and liked the process of learning in shop class, but the food in home economics, and the potential game-making in computer programming took me away from wood shop. Nonetheless, I continued to create and make long after high school.

As a high school teacher, I began to see a divide between the kids who took shop class and often went to the local technical school and those students who took all "academic" classes. This is not to say that the students in this class weren't academic. We had fantastic discussions in English class where we consistently made high-level connections, yet many of the students who were in this "lower-level class" did not see themselves as academic and wanted to do other things after high school. In fact, many thought high school was a waste of their time because it had "nothing to do" with where they were headed.

I loved the real-world perspective many of these students brought to my class, but I hated the fact that I categorized them as "those students" (meaning tech-school students). The other piece was how the percentages were swayed heavily to boys in both our shop classes and technical school. I mean 90 percent boys and 10 percent girls heavy!

The flipside of this equation was a set of students who took every advanced placement (AP) and honors-level class they could take during their high school journey. Their goals for high school were different. They wanted to get into a great college and knew they had to have a high school resume that would reflect how intelligent and hardworking they had been for the past four years.

They rarely did anything with their hands that was not tied to a set of standards or written out on paper. This was not to say they weren't creative. Far from it. It's just that their academic path limited their opportunities for "making."

If Only It Were That Simple

Like most things in life, school—for me as a teenager and, later, as a teacher—was not cut and dry. Most students don't fall into either of the above paths. I fell somewhere in between, shying away from AP classes yet also not seeing the value in tech school.

But I was always tinkering around, making videos (before everyone made videos) and writing my own songs and recording them. I was always interested in music, and I was part of a band. At the time, I didn't know I was a "maker." I did know that when something interested me I usually jumped at the chance to play with it and learn more about it.

As a teacher, it took a while for the "maker" in me to come out during my job. I was trying to figure out what a teacher was *supposed to do* in my first few years before I finally connected my personal passions with the art of teaching.

When I gave my students the choice to work on whatever project they wanted for our 20% Time projects, I joined in the fun. I decided to build my own app from scratch (something I had always wanted to do) and the maker in me came out again.

During this time, I saw my students struggle with their projects—and push through. Even though the projects were not tied to grades, the kids still cared and had a higher level of commitment than I could have ever drawn out with a quiz or test.

This was English class, and we were making things with our hands. We were also writing, reading, speaking, and sharing about our own projects and listening to the other students talk about their projects.

Although my students and I embodied the maker mindset during those forty-five minutes each week, the problem was simple: That was not enough time.

They needed more experiences in school, like 20% Time, where they could fail safely, learn by tinkering, collaborate freely, and see an idea go from seed to creation over a period of time.

Why This Needs to Change in the Twenty-First Century

Yes, we are more than fifteen years into the twenty-first century and keep talking about it like we're still not living in this world. We all know how the world has changed, and how our students have changed—not to mention how the workforce has and will continue to shift toward jobs that require critical thinking, communication, collaboration, and creativity.

But I still see many schools as silos. If you want to go to college, take this path; and if you want to get "career ready" take this other path over here. That's not going to cut it anymore.

The career-ready path has to have strong academic merit to it, just as the college-ready path must have creative merit to it for them to actually prepare students for life after school.

Shouldn't a student who is heading to college to take engineering courses have hands-on experience designing, making, and building in school? Shouldn't a student who is starting their own landscaping or design business after graduation have experience writing business plans, speaking to an audience, and connecting their math class to their business interests? And shouldn't an elementary student interested in everything have the opportunity to explore with their mind and their hands as they make their way through our K–12 system?

As a teacher, parent, and student myself, I believe we need to expect more out of all of our students, and give them the opportunities in school to do real work instead of consistently preparing them for whatever comes next.

BEYOND MAKERSPACES: CREATING A MAKER DEPARTMENT

I (A.J.) met Dan for the first time this summer and was immediately impressed by his knowledge and attitude toward teaching and learning. He was a tech-ed teacher in Upper Perkiomen School District where I was the new administrator. We were on the same interview panel for new teachers and got to know each other quickly.

Dan had a wide range of experiences teaching every level of tech-ed and industrial arts within the district. He had been at the elementary school and middle school and had made the switch back to the high school this summer.

We got into a discussion during our first meeting about the changing landscape of high school and how the industrial arts department and program needed a redesign. **By September, our idea had transformed into something tangible, as we understood this challenge and gathered research to support our idea (Phase 1).**

We set out to create a new ninth-grade course where students would have the opportunity to learn design and engineering concepts hands on through a variety of creative experiences. We also wanted to create a course that would be gender neutral in its description and experiences, hopefully bringing the ratio between boys and girls in class closer to 50/50.

After meeting with the high school principals, our assistant to the superintendent, our area robotics expert, and the other members of the department, **we began to put together the pieces of this course to frame the opportunity for our students and school (Phase 2).**

With the challenge, idea, and opportunity firmly in place, our **next steps were meeting with various stakeholders and then going back to the drawing board again and again (Phase 3).**

We decided this course had to be a funnel for the rest of the department's offerings. We couldn't have all the ninth graders take a design and engineering course, only to take traditional wood shop courses in tenth, eleventh, and twelfth grades. We also wanted to make sure we kept the good pieces of our industrial arts program instead of throwing out everything.

Our refined course idea looked like this:

Course: Creative Design and Engineering

This course will provide students with an active hands-on learning environment that promotes a higher level of thinking through real life problem-solving situations while brainstorming, modeling, and collaborating in a team environment. Together, students will form a foundation to help them succeed in an ever changing society.

The course will have four specific modules:

1. Robotics
2. Build and Manufacture
3. Product Creation
4. Design

As we got more and more feedback, we redesigned the entire flow of offerings and courses in our IA department (Phase 4):

Impact: The Entire Program

9th Grade: Creative Design and Engineering (students are introduced to three different pathways)

Robotics & Programming Pathway Courses

1. Robotics Programming and Sensors
2. Robotic Manipulation and Problem Solving
3. Team Competition
4. Robotic Innovations

Design Pathway Courses

1. Graphic Design

2. Environmental Power

3. Architectural and Interior Design

4. Design & Prototyping Innovations

Engineering Pathway Courses

1. Manufacturing

2. Product Design and Development

3. Set Design

4. Entrepreneurship and Design

We named our course Creative Design and Engineering. It allows students to make, create, and build in four different areas:

- Students compete in a head-to-head robotics competition while learning the principles of design, construction, and programming.

- Students construct a fully functioning desk clock that demonstrates the creative concepts that go into the building process.

- Students are given the task of creating a product for daily use in their life, designing it in AutoCAD, and printing using a 3-D printer (i.e., iPhone Case).

- Students will design and create their own personal logo that will be cut on a vinyl plotter and placed on an article of clothing or other graphic product of their choice.

For students to have these experiences, we had to propose the new course to our school board along with the budget requests to make this a possibility.

We needed the following equipment to make it all happen:

- Vex Robotics team set for students to build out their own robots in each class and then create a competition where teams of robots played against each other.

- 3-D printers from Airwolf: We searched far and wide and felt this line of three-dimensional printers were perfect for our new course and department.

- 4x8 CNC Router to allow students to design and create professional grade products for our community and school district: Our students would be able to create their own custom products with almost any material.

- Vinyl Cutter/Plotter, which is versatile and allows for a wide variety of finished products that include shirt logos, magnets, decals, signage, and other creative media.

- Heat Press to be used along with the vinyl cutter for our design aspect of the course.

We presented our proposal to our school board and had a good amount of questions about the course and direction in which we were headed. The following week they unanimously voted for our course approval and budget requests!

More importantly, **we wanted all ninth graders to have this opportunity and allow their feedback and interests to continue to drive our course creation in the upper grade levels (Phase 5).**

Expanding Design Thinking and Making Beyond the One Department

You may have noticed the **bold text** above with Phases 1-5 listed. We lived the LAUNCH Cycle throughout this process. But it wasn't complete. Imagine if we had stopped right there, gotten the equipment, and assumed we were finished. We began to Highlight the work (Phase 6) that our students were doing in this course and expanded it to other areas.

In January of 2016, our school district began planning and preparation for a TEDx event we planned to host at our high school that May. We had more than twenty teachers, plus nine administrators and fifty students, all playing major roles as part of our TEDxPennsburgED planning committee! We were going to LAUNCH this event together, with multiple people contributing and making this an event to remember. Some top moments from the event included:

- Our teachers, students, and custodial staff completely revitalized our courtyard area for a reception after the event, installing a pond, landscaping the area, planting perennials and annuals, and setting it up for our guests.

- Our teachers and students at the high school built the set for the stage (it's so awesome). They've made the TEDx letters, signs, and so much more. Using our 3-D printers and CNC routers, the students who were in the new classes spent time during and after school to get the stage looking professional.

- We had a group of students from our elementary school showcasing apps and games they'd made with MIT App Creator and Scratch during the intermission time period; our local robotics club put on a show during intermission, and students from our middle school and high school demonstrated the things they made on a daily basis with computers, 3-D printers, CNC routers, and much more!

- Our play director and high school English teacher (she's fantastic) took the lead on fleshing out many of the details and brought the stage crew and production team from the school play on board to create a schedule and take care of our speakers before, during, and after the event.

- Our high school television-lab students set up the entire audio and visual aspects of the TEDx event. They did the first-ever live stream from Upper Perkiomen High School so people around the world could watch the event on our website in real time with multiple camera angles being edited on the fly.

This TEDx event took us through the entire LAUNCH Cycle and ended with a full-out launch where students created, marketed, and sold their ideas and production to a huge, authentic audience.

As one student said after the event, "Now, that was a rush!"

When you take students through the entire cycle and have them launch what they've made and believe in, something magical happens that we don't see every day: They feel proud. They feel accomplished. They feel like they've made a mark on the world.

Better yet, they are inspired. Inspired by one another. Inspired by their work. Inspired by sharing it with a real audience. Inspired by what they did and launched.

When we talk about design thinking, creativity, innovation, and the maker movement, we can't forget to remember what's most important: giving students the opportunity to make an impact right now. Not tomorrow. Not next year. Not when they graduate. *Right now.*

LAUNCHING YOUR STORY OUT INTO THE WORLD

We started this book by writing a manifesto. We shared our beliefs, our hopes, and our dreams for a better future of teaching and learning. We also shared the reason we wrote this book in the first place. It's because of you: The teacher, school leader, or parent who is working with kids every day. You have the power to inspire, empower, and embolden a generation of makers and innovators. And in turn, they will inspire you and each other.

This book is our story, but it is also the story of so many teachers and students who are making, designing, building, and creating right now in classrooms around the world. We saw this first hand on April 26, 2016.

The Global Day of Design started off as an idea we had to jumpstart design thinking in schools from every part of the world. We looked around and listened to teachers who wanted a day to celebrate creativity.

We asked what this might look like in a classroom. *Should it be one day, one hour, or one week?* As we began to collect ideas and responses online, the idea morphed into something tangible.

The Global Day of Design would give teachers and students an opportunity to do a Design Challenge or Maker Project. Design Challenges took a few hours of class time, while Maker Projects were shorter at around an hour of class time.

We put up the website GlobalDayOfDesign.com and added twenty design challenges and maker projects for teachers to use in their classrooms. We shared it out with a few people to get feedback and changed the hashtag (#GDD16) and a few other items on the site.

Then it was time to LAUNCH!

We didn't know what to expect. It was one of those scary moments of putting an idea out into the world and seeing how the world responds.

What happened next speaks to all of the creative teachers and educators currently working with children.

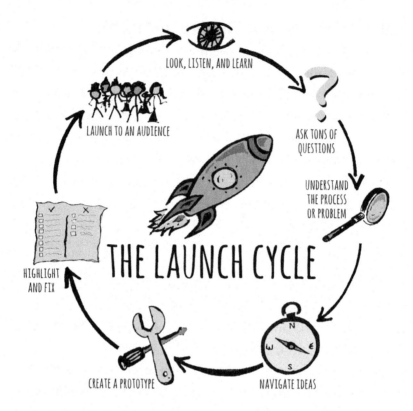

LOOK, LISTEN, AND LEARN

ASK TONS OF QUESTIONS

UNDERSTAND THE PROCESS OR PROBLEM

LAUNCH TO AN AUDIENCE

HIGHLIGHT AND FIX

THE LAUNCH CYCLE

CREATE A PROTOTYPE

NAVIGATE IDEAS

We saw teachers from around the world sign up their classrooms to participate in The Global Day of Design. We received e-mails, tweets, and messages with new design challenge ideas, sample maker projects for other classrooms to use, and ideas to spread the word to every part of the world.

By April 26th, 2016 there were over 450 schools and 40,000 students from 13 different countries participating in The Global Day of Design!

Students led the charge, sharing their creations on Twitter, Facebook, Instagram, Snapchat, and Periscope using the hashtag #GDD16. Teachers supported, empowered, and designed alongside students throughout the day, inspiring others to join along at the last minute.

It was a reminder that while we have a major impact on our students' lives every day as a teacher, our students also have the ability to impact our lives and the lives of their peers when given the opportunity.

When we LAUNCH, students have the opportunity to be the change they wish to see in the world. They know that their voice counts, their work matters, and their passion can be contagious.

How can we possibly take that opportunity away from them? Today, right now, pledge to LAUNCH with your students. You won't regret it. Because if one thing is true, it's this: Our impact is not always what we say or what we do, but instead what we empower our students to say and do while they are in our classrooms—so they can make a dent in the universe right now and always.

Visit TheLaunchCycle.com/launch to get more information and resources on the last phase of the LAUNCH Cycle. Join the discussion online using the hashtag #launchbook.

FAQ
Frequently Asked Questions

What Should I Do First?

Design projects can seem daunting at first. Your best option might be to start out small, perhaps with a project that will last a week or two. You could keep the research section shorter and focus more on the creating portion. Or you might do a little less planning in the Navigating Ideas phase. Ultimately, you are the expert. You know your class better than anyone else. You know what your students need. We provided a flexible framework that you can modify to fit the needs of your classroom.

You might want to pilot your design project with a specific group. If you teach multiple classes, use it as an experiment and try it with just one group. Compare the engagement levels of the design thinking unit and the traditional unit. Pay attention to your students' skill development. Is it better or worse than a traditional unit? What about student engagement? How has it changed?

You might also want to partner with another class in your building. Sometimes it helps to have a group with which you can lean on. You are doing something bold and risky and different. This can be exhausting. But having a trusted colleague or, better yet, a trusted team can make all the difference.

How Do I Get My Students, Parents, and Administration On Board?

I (John) remember feeling terrified the first time that my class launched a design project. The process seemed slower than a typical unit plan. Instead of a one-week project or a single assignment, students worked for weeks on their products. Rather than delivering the typical *I do, we do, you do* lesson, we mixed things up with students spending more time working while I met with small groups and individuals.

It was more active, more chaotic, and at times more confusing than an orderly classroom. After all, we were exploring. We were heading to the moon. And doing so meant we had to take risks.

I was okay with these risks, but I had several days when I worried about what certain stakeholders would think. What would administrators think? Would they worry that our class would fall behind on standardized test scores? Would they see the chaos and think that I had failed in classroom management? What about parents? Would they say, "Back when I was a kid, we didn't waste time with stuff like this"? Would they find this project bizarre? Would they understand that we were doing less work but deeper thinking?

You can be proactive by communicating with stakeholders ahead of time. This way, nobody is surprised that your class suddenly seems different. Instead, they understand the rationale for what you are doing, and they have a vision for where you are going. You might want to consider the following things before you begin a design thinking project with your class:

- What concerns will stakeholders have? How do you answer their concerns?

- What type of research can you find to back up the success of design thinking?

- What skills will students gain as a result of this design project?

- How is this aligned to the curriculum?

- What rules will you have in place to guarantee success?

- How is design thinking used outside of the school context?

- What are some things that will remain the same? Parents and administrators should know what types of structures will remain the same.

As you think about communication, consider how you will convey the purpose, the research, and the process in a way that supports student learning. Focus on how this will benefit children and how it will lead to deeper learning. Convey this information in a way that is celebratory rather than cautionary.

It's important to send out this communication ahead of time. It might be a series of phone calls, a conversation at Meet the Teacher Night, a newsletter, an e-mail, or a video you create and send out. Don't stop there, though. As you progress through your design project, think of ways that you can share the great things that students are doing in class. Take pictures or videos of the projects and share them on social media. Invite decision makers from the district office or the school board. Be a leader in a new way of learning within your school. When your design projects are done, share the experience. Show the student work along with reflections of what your class learned in the process.

This might seem like boasting. It might feel arrogant. We, as teachers, can be reluctant to share the great things that are happening in our classrooms. However, it's something we should celebrate. Going to the moon was an accomplishment. And when a child does something wildly creative—even if it didn't turn out perfectly—that is just as much of an accomplishment.

Celebrating was always the weakest area for me. I (John) never knew how to have a celebration about a mural or a documentary or a group of Scratch video games. I was so scared that people might be disappointed and that students would feel the same way. So, for a decade, I failed to celebrate our design projects.

I now realize that there's a place to share what didn't work. A celebration of learning is just that—a celebration. It's a chance to say, "Yes, we failed. But we learned. We learned a ton even when this wasn't perfect." It's a chance to tell the story realistically in a way that allows people to say, "I could do that. I could definitely do that."

What about the Curriculum Map?

You might be looking at the design thinking cycle and wondering how you are supposed to accomplish this given your curriculum map. However, design thinking isn't meant to be something you squeeze in before or after a traditional unit. It's not a culminating project. It is a different way of organizing the curriculum.

Design thinking is meant to be a flexible framework. You do not need to transform your entire classroom into a design classroom and abandon all other best practices. Nor do you need to take time out of the standards to create a separate space for design thinking. Design projects should work as an integrated part of the curriculum you already teach. Just as you would organize a typical unit with a specific framework and a set of strategies, you can use the design thinking cycle as a new framework with specific strategies that will support the standards you already use.

So how exactly do you do this?

The first thing to consider is the standards that fit best with the design thinking framework. For example, in a language arts class, you might want to connect it to the reading standards in research, the writing standards with functional, expository, and persuasive texts. Or if students are using design thinking for a NaNoWriMo novel project, you could focus on the narrative standards while also adding informational reading standards within the research process.

It helps to find standards that will allow students to actually make something. In math, you might tie in all of the standards in statistics and probability into a board-game-design project. However, you might find that integers simply don't work as well with the concept of design. The idea here is to avoid standards where the work students are doing is loosely connected to the standards.

Sometimes it's hard to justify spending a longer period of time on a project that seems to connect to just one standard. Here's where the idea of chunking and connecting comes in. If a subject has a few specific concept standards that fit in nicely within a unit, chunk those together as the central focus of your design projects. Next, look at all of the skill standards that fit within the stages of design thinking. You might be surprised by just how many standards connect to it.

In some cases, you might run into rigid curriculum maps. A school might say, "You need to teach inferencing this week," or "You need to teach persuasive texts these seven days." While it's important to follow the map, remember that maps are just that—guides to inspire possibilities, rather than routes to tell you exactly what to do. This is where you can add additional connecting standards while highlighting the focus standard for that particular week. Very few principals will say, "Only teach this standard and nothing else."

SHOULD I ASSESS THE PRODUCT OR THE PROCESS?

When doing design projects, teachers will often ask, "Should I assess the finished product or the process?" The short answer is "both and neither." See, there is value in having students self-assess their creative process in the design cycle. For example, they might look at brainstorming or researching and rate how well they were able to accomplish those tasks. Similarly, there is value in looking at the finished product and seeing if it is truly a viable product for the final audience.

That said, the goal is for students to master the standards that you are teaching. While we advocate for self-assessment in both the process and the product, the greater question is, "How does this work demonstrate mastery of standards?" We use the following Standards-Based Grid as a way for students to know exactly what standards they are mastering.

The way this works is simple. The teacher takes the standards that are associated with the design project and lists all learning targets in student-friendly terms. As students progress through the project, teachers fill out formative feedback in the Mastery Level category while also listing corresponding evidence and teacher feedback. Then, during student conferences (described in the next section), students are able to add their own feedback.

Standards-Based Assessment Grid

Subject:

Quarter:

Prerequisite Skills:

1. I can _____

2. I can _____

3. I can _____

Level of Mastery

Learning Target (Aligned to Standard)	Mastery Level	Corresponding Evidence	Teacher Feedback	Student Feedback
I can distinguish between theoretical and experimental probability.	Exceeds	T-Chart, Research Facts, Concept Map, Board Game Rationale	You were able to demonstrate the difference between theoretical and experimental probability during the Board Game Project.	I proved that I understand all the ways that both sides had to prepare for a Total War and I showed examples for each area.

WHAT SHOULD A DESIGN PROJECT HAVE?

At its most basic, you should think through the following ahead of time:

- **Standards:** What standards connect best with design thinking? Are there specific standards that most naturally draw out student creativity? Are there standards that you can chunk together to create a cohesive unit?

- **Product:** What is the ultimate product that students will create? Remember that a product can be an action. It might mean a service project in social studies or a theater production you create in language arts.

- **Timing:** When is the best time of year to do your design thinking project? When are students going to be the most receptive? When, in your school culture, does it seem to be safest to take risks? In other words, if there is a heavy pressure connected to upcoming standardized tests, it might work best to do a design project afterward. Also think about how long it will take to do a design project. A good rule of thumb is to create a framework and then add 20 percent to the allotted time. It's not uncommon for interruptions to derail a schedule.

- **Materials:** What types of materials will you need to find? Where will you store the materials? How will students access them?

- **Management:** What types of changes will you need to make in classroom management? What types of rules and procedures will you need to develop? How will you teach these to students?

- **Knowledge:** What type of knowledge do you still need? Where will you find that knowledge? Who are some people to whom you can talk?

- **Collaborators:** Design thinking projects can feel overwhelming. However, sometimes it helps to think about potential collaborators who can go through the process with you. Who are some trusted colleagues with whom you can work?

LAUNCH LESSON PLANS

Here's a quick explanation of the features in the lesson plans that follow:

 ## LESSON PREVIEW

- **Lesson Topic**: This is the main idea for the lesson.

- **LAUNCH Cycle Phases**: Occasionally, a lesson will involve multiple parts of the LAUNCH Cycle. So we list the specific phases here.

- **Estimated Time**: This is merely an estimation. Times will vary according to your specific students.

- **Objectives**: These objectives are designed to be clear, concise, and student friendly while also connecting to depths of knowledge and Bloom's Taxonomy.

- **Common Core Standards**: We connect each lesson to the Common Core Standards.

- **Vocabulary**: We include student-friendly definitions for any academic language that might be tricky for students.

 ## LESSON PREPARATION

- **Materials**: This is a list of any materials you will need for that specific lesson.

- **Tasks**: This is a list of tasks that you will need to do before beginning the lesson.

LESSON OUTLINE

Slide #	Teacher Tasks	Student Tasks
Each slide has a number at the bottom right-hand corner. This section explains where you should be in the slide-show.	This is a short explanation of what you, as a teacher, will be doing during this part of the lesson.	This is a short explanation of what your students will be doing during this part of the lesson.

LESSON ONE

 ## LESSON PREVIEW

Lesson Topic
Exploring the Design Thinking Challenge

LAUNCH Cycle Phases
Phase One: Look, Listen, and Learn

Estimated Time
60-75 minutes

Objectives

- I can define my audience.

- I can create an audience survey and display the results in a graph.

Common Core Standards

CCSS.ELA-LITERACY.RI.5.7
Draw on information from multiple print or digital sources, demonstrating the ability to locate an answer to a question quickly or to solve a problem efficiently.

CCSS.ELA-LITERACY.W.5.10
Write routinely over extended time frames (time for research, reflection, and revision) and shorter time frames (a single sitting or a day or two) for a range of discipline-specific tasks, purposes, and audiences.

CCSS.ELA-LITERACY.SL.5.1

Engage effectively in a range of collaborative discussions (one-on-one, in groups, and teacher-led) with diverse partners on grade 5 topics and texts, building on others' ideas and expressing their own clearly.

Vocabulary

- **Design Thinking**: a structured way of thinking creatively

- **LAUNCH Cycle**: a framework for design thinking

- **Audience**: the people for whom you will design your product (in this case a roller coaster)

- **Survey**: questions you will ask your audience

- **Data**: information you are gathering

- **Trend**: things that seem to be happening often

 LESSON PREPARATION

Materials

Each LAUNCH team should have:

- ☐ Duct Tape

- ☐ Paper

- ☐ Cardboard

- ☐ A Marble

- ☐ Plastic Straws

- ☐ Popsicle Sticks

- [ ] Each student should have the LAUNCH Notebook

- [ ] Each student will need a 3x5 card

- [ ] Optional: colored pencils for the graphing portion of the lesson

Preparation Tasks

- Make sure to set up the classroom in a way that facilitates collaboration.

- Make sure to fill each box with the necessary supplies.

- Make sure that you have set up the slideshow.

 LESSON OUTLINE

Slide #	Teacher Tasks	Student Tasks
1-4	Pass out the LAUNCH Notebooks and instruct students to go to page one. Show the Design Challenge Video.	Watch the video and jot down any questions you have in the first page of your LAUNCH Notebook.
5	Break the students up into their LAUNCH team groups.	Go to your assigned LAUNCH team. Share any questions you have in the form of a round-robin.
6-14	Go over the LAUNCH Cycle with your students. Keep this quick and to the point. You might want to include the video explaining the cycle.	Listen to the LAUNCH Cycle. It is also included in your LAUNCH Notebook.

15-17	Instruct the LAUNCH teams to create their survey questions. Walk around the class to see if their questions are on task and relate to the design challenge.	As a group, create a list of four questions you would like to ask your audience. Feel free to use the sentence stems provided if you are struggling with what to ask. Each member should have each question listed in his or her LAUNCH Notebook.
18	Instruct students to divvy up the questions so that each student gets one question.	Next, divide up the questions so that each student gets one question.
No slide (use white-board)	Model how to turn a survey question into a multiple-choice survey question. You can use the sample given or you can create one of your own.	Watch the teacher's example. Think about how you will turn your survey question into a multiple-choice question.
19	Monitor the class and answer any questions they have about the survey.	Survey each of your classmates using the options you created. Make sure to write your data in the table in your LAUNCH Notebook.
20	Instruct the students to sit back at their original spots and create the graphs.	Individually, create a bar graph or a circle graph demonstrating the data.
21	Monitor the groups to make sure that they are describing trends that they see. You might need to explain the concept of a trend to a few students.	Share your results with your LAUNCH team. What trends do you notice? What kinds of opinions do your classmates have about roller coasters?

22-23	Use this time to have fun with your students. As they play around with the supplies, you might want to join them.	Take some time to explore your items. You don't need to write anything here. Just play around with them. What are some of the possibilities that you see? What are some design ideas that you might want to test out as you build a roller coaster?
24	Pass out 3x5 cards. As students leave, collect the exit slips.	Closure: Exit Slips What is one question you still have? What is one thing you learned? What do you hope to do tomorrow?

LESSON TWO

 ## LESSON PREVIEW

Lesson Topic
Exploring How Roller Coasters Work

LAUNCH Cycle Phases
Phase Two: Ask Tons of Questions
Phase Three: Understand the Problem or Process (in this case, how to create a roller coaster)

Estimated Time
45-60 minutes

Objectives

- I can generate inquiry questions.

- I can engage in online research by asking questions, analyzing information, and summarizing the answers in my own words.

Common Core Standards

CCSS.ELA-LITERACY.RI.5.2
Determine two or more main ideas of a text and explain how they are supported by key details; summarize the text.

CCSS.ELA-LITERACY.RI.5.3
Explain the relationships or interactions between two or more individuals, events, ideas, or concepts in a historical, scientific, or technical text based on specific information in the text.

CCSS.ELA-LITERACY.RI.5.7

Draw on information from multiple print or digital sources, demonstrating the ability to locate an answer to a question quickly or to solve a problem efficiently.

CCSS.ELA-LITERACY.W.5.9

Draw evidence from literary or informational texts to support analysis, reflection, and research.

CCSS.ELA-LITERACY.W.5.10

Write routinely over extended time frames (time for research, reflection, and revision) and shorter time frames (a single sitting or a day or two) for a range of discipline-specific tasks, purposes, and audiences.

CCSS.ELA-LITERACY.SL.5.1

Engage effectively in a range of collaborative discussions (one-on-one, in groups, and teacher-led) with diverse partners on grade 5 topics and texts, building on others' ideas and expressing their own clearly.

Vocabulary

- **Inquiry**: questions that come from your own curiosity

- **Analyze**: examine information carefully

- **Generate**: to create

 ## LESSON PREPARATION

Materials

☐ Each group needs chart paper and markers.

☐ Each student should have the LAUNCH Notebook.

☐ Each student will need a 3x5 card.

☐ Optional: you may or may not want to allow the box of materials to be available.

Preparation Tasks

- Make sure to set up the classroom in a way that facilitates collaboration.

- Make sure that you have set up the slideshow.

LESSON OUTLINE

Slide #	Teacher Tasks	Student Tasks
25-28	Have students get out their LAUNCH Notebooks and begin the first individual task.	Individually: What kinds of questions do you have about how roller coasters work?
29	Rotate around the room and check to see that students are showing empathy toward their audience.	As a team, go round-robin and share your questions. As you add your questions to chart paper, individually add any additional questions that your group came up with in your LAUNCH Notebook.
30	As the students do the carousel activity, consider pulling aside any students who have struggled in the last step. See if there is any way you could help them see the perspective of the audience. *Note: You may want to time the carousel activity and have a signal to switch. However, you may also want to allow your students to walk around at their own pace.*	Do a carousel activity where your LAUNCH team looks at the questions of other LAUNCH teams and individually adds additional questions to your own LAUNCH Notebooks.

None	Model how to look for different roller coasters and how to find examples of how they work.	Watch how your teacher models the research process.
31-33	Pull aside any struggling readers who might have a hard time with the research process.	Take your questions and begin researching online how roller coasters work. You might be curious what makes the tracks work or how they can continue to move from start to finish or how they go through a loop. Make sure to write your question, summarize your answer, and cite your source. Add the answers to your chart.
34	Monitor the class during the phase to see that they have a clear concept in their mind of what it will take to create a great roller coaster.	Individually: Sketch out some ideas for your roller coaster.
35	Pass out 3x5 cards. As students leave, collect the exit slips.	Closure: Exit Slips What are some roller coaster ideas that you have? List any of the ideas on this card.

Lesson Three

Lesson Preview

Lesson Topic
Navigating Ideas and Planning Out the Roller Coaster

LAUNCH Cycle Phases
Phase Four: Navigate Ideas

Estimated Time
45-60 minutes

Objectives

- I can create a web demonstrating all the criteria in a roller coaster.

- I can generate ideas of potential roller coasters.

- I can analyze and combine ideas to create a plan for a new roller coaster.

Common Core Standards

CCSS.ELA-LITERACY.RI.5.9
Integrate information from several texts on the same topic in order to write or speak about the subject knowledgeably.

CCSS.ELA-LITERACY.W.5.10
Write routinely over extended time frames (time for research, reflection, and revision) and shorter time frames (a single sitting or a day or two) for a range of discipline-specific tasks, purposes, and audiences.

CCSS.ELA-LITERACY.SL.5.1

Engage effectively in a range of collaborative discussions (one-on-one, in groups, and teacher-led) with diverse partners on grade 5 topics and texts, building on others' ideas and expressing their own clearly.

Vocabulary

- **Navigate**: to explore

- **Criteria**: the elements needed to make something

 LESSON PREPARATION

Materials

- ☐ Each group needs chart paper and markers.

- ☐ Each student should have the LAUNCH Notebook.

- ☐ Each student will need a 3x5 card.

- ☐ Optional: you may or may not want to allow the box of materials to be available.

Preparation Tasks

- Make sure to set up the classroom in a way that facilitates collaboration.

- Make sure that you have set up the slideshow.

LESSON OUTLINE

Slide #	Teacher Tasks	Student Tasks
36-38	Check to see that students are connecting the concept of questions to the idea of a web. If necessary, model this process for your students.	Individual: Create a web showing all the things that a great roller coaster might have.
39	Pay close attention to each LAUNCH team and their ability to think connectively about this topic.	LAUNCH team: Share your ideas in one larger brainstorm. This could be a list or a web on chart paper. Make sure each group member gets a chance to add ideas.
40	Number the students from 1-4 in each group. Have student #1 move counter-clockwise to the next group and student #4 move clockwise to the next group.	Once the groups are joined together, take a look at the brainstorm and offer any additional ideas they might be missing.
41	Have the students return to their groups.	Share any insights you have from interacting with other groups. What ideas might you want to consider?
42	Walk around the groups to monitor how they are interacting. You might have some students arguing over ideas, so this is a chance to navigate any potential conflict.	Create your one main concept as a group. Students will draw their roller coaster concepts individually in their LAUNCH Notebooks.

43	Pass out 3x5 cards. As students leave, collect the exit slips.	Closure: Exit Slips How well did your group work together? Did you feel like people listened to your ideas? Why or why not?

LESSON FOUR

 ## LESSON PREVIEW

Lesson Topic
Creating Your Roller Coaster

LAUNCH Cycle Phases
Phase Five: Create
Phase Six: Highlight What's Working and Fix What's Failing

Estimated Time
60-90 minutes

Note that you may want to spend multiple days on this particular lesson. Sometimes the making process is slow, messy, and time-consuming. But it's totally worth it!

Objectives

- I can work with my team to create a prototype of my roller coaster.

- I can create an annotated visual of my team's roller coaster.

- I can test and revise my prototype by highlighting what's working and fix what's failing.

Common Core Standards

CCSS.ELA-LITERACY.W.5.10

Write routinely over extended time frames (time for research, reflection, and revision) and shorter time frames (a single sitting or a day or two) for a range of discipline-specific tasks, purposes, and audiences.

CCSS.ELA-LITERACY.SL.5.1

Engage effectively in a range of collaborative discussions (one-on-one, in groups, and teacher-led) with diverse partners on grade 5 topics and texts, building on others' ideas and expressing their own clearly.

Vocabulary

- **Prototype**: an initial version of what you've created

- **Revise**: to improve

- **Annotate**: add a written description on top of the visual explaining it

 ## LESSON PREPARATION

Materials

Each LAUNCH team should have:

- ☐ Duct Tape

- ☐ Paper

- ☐ Cardboard

- ☐ A Marble

- ☐ Plastic Straws

- ☐ Popsicle Sticks

- ☐ Each student should have the LAUNCH Notebook.

Preparation Tasks

- Make sure to set up the classroom in a way that facilitates collaboration.

- Make sure that you have cleared out a space (perhaps outside) where students can actually create their roller coasters.

- Make sure to fill each box with the necessary supplies.

- Make sure that you have set up the slideshow.

 LESSON OUTLINE

Slide #	Teacher Tasks	Student Tasks
44-47	Watch the group dynamics to see how they are collaborating. When most groups have created an initial concept, move to the next stage in the lesson (and the next phase in the LAUNCH Cycle).	LAUNCH team: Start creating your roller coaster. Have fun with this part.
48-51	Encourage students to test by playing. Let them make mistakes and improve with each iteration.	Spend some time playing with it. Jot down what's working and not working in the table of your LAUNCH Notebook.
52	Pass out 3x5 cards. As students leave, collect the exit slips.	Closure: Exit Slips Is your group ready to launch your roller coaster to the classroom? Why or why not?

LESSON FIVE

 ## LESSON PREVIEW

Lesson Topic
Launching It!

LAUNCH Cycle Phases
Phase Seven: Launch It to the World!

Estimated Time
60 minutes

Objectives

- I can create directions that other students can follow.

- I can convince people that this would be a great roller coaster.

Common Core Standards

CCSS.ELA-LITERACY.RI.5.9
Integrate information from several texts on the same topic in order to write or speak about the subject knowledgeably.

CCSS.ELA-LITERACY.W.5.2
Write informative/explanatory texts to examine a topic and convey ideas and information clearly.

CCSS.ELA-LITERACY.W.5.6

With some guidance and support from adults, use technology, including the Internet, to produce and publish writing as well as to interact and collaborate with others; demonstrate sufficient command of keyboarding skills to type a minimum of two pages in a single sitting.

CCSS.ELA-LITERACY.W.5.10

Write routinely over extended time frames (time for research, reflection, and revision) and shorter time frames (a single sitting or a day or two) for a range of discipline-specific tasks, purposes, and audiences.

CCSS.ELA-LITERACY.SL.5.1

Engage effectively in a range of collaborative discussions (one-on-one, in groups, and teacher-led) with diverse partners on grade 5 topics and texts, building on others' ideas and expressing their own clearly.

CCSS.ELA-LITERACY.SL.5.4

Report on a topic or text or present an opinion, sequencing ideas logically and using appropriate facts and relevant, descriptive details to support main ideas or themes; speak clearly at an understandable pace.

CCSS.ELA-LITERACY.SL.5.5

Include multimedia components (e.g., graphics, sound) and visual displays in presentations when appropriate to enhance the development of main ideas or themes.

LESSON PREPARATION

Materials

Each LAUNCH team should have:

- ☐ Duct Tape

- ☐ Paper

- ☐ Cardboard

- ☐ A Marble

- ☐ Plastic Straws

- ☐ Popsicle Sticks

- ☐ Each student should have the LAUNCH Notebook.

Preparation Tasks

- Make sure to set up the classroom in a way that facilitates collaboration.

- Make sure that you have cleared out a space (perhaps outside) where students can demonstrate how their roller coaster works.

- Make sure to fill each box with the necessary supplies.

- Make sure that you have set up the slideshow.

LESSON OUTLINE

Slide #	Teacher Tasks	Student Tasks
53-54	Monitor the class and gauge whether or not they might need some more time in the last phase of the LAUNCH Cycle.	Pair-Share: Is your roller coaster ready to launch? What modifications would you make?
55-56	This is your chance to hype them up for the launch. It's okay to go downright silly in this moment. In other words, play "The Final Countdown" and sing along. Or don't. It's your choice. Explain that the launch is about to happen.	Listen to the instructions.
57	Listen to students think strategically about their launch.	Groups discuss their strategies for how they will reach their audience.

| 58 | Work with any groups that need help on how to create their launch products. | Now that you have finished with the roller coaster, you will launch the ride to your classmates.

Option 1: Create a list of instructions showing how the roller coaster works.

Option 2: Create a list of instructions with pictures showing how the roller coaster works.

Option 3: Create a video showing how the roller coaster works.

Option 4: Create an advertisement for the roller coaster.

Option 5: Create a step-by-step storyboard showing what it would be like to ride your roller coaster. |
| --- | --- | --- |
| 59 | Play with each group and use this as a chance to celebrate what they've created. | Gallery Walk for the roller coasters. Have one student stay back to demonstrate the coaster while other groups go from group to group. |
| 60 | Guide students through the self-reflection stage. | Optional: Self-reflection questions |

LAUNCH NOTEBOOK
CREATE A ROLLER COASTER

Design Challenges

You're going to make something amazing, and you're going to start on it today. It's going to be something that has never existed before in the history of humanity.

You know how you typically turn in an assignment to your teacher and then you get it back and, well, that's pretty much it. This is different. Working with your design team, you're going to create something people will actually use!

The LAUNCH Process

Look all around you. Seriously. Glance around your classroom. You are surrounded by things that people created. Not only did they create these things, but they also designed them. The fancy term for this is design thinking. It's the term professionals use. You're going to use the LAUNCH Process. It's a modified version of the design thinking cycle that artists and engineers use in the real world. Here's how it works:

Look, Listen, and Learn

Ask a Ton of Questions

Understand the Problem or Process

Navigate the Ideas

Create a Prototype

Highlight What's Working and Fix What's Failing

Ready to Launch!

Phase One:
Look, Listen, and Learn

LOOK AT THE CHALLENGE

Watch the video and listen closely to the challenge.

You're going to build the ultimate roller coaster. Okay, you're not actually going to build a life-size roller coaster that you can ride. Apparently, there's this thing called safety that schools have to follow. Bummer. But you are going to design and build a model of a roller coaster. It needs to be the kind of roller coaster someone would actually enjoy.

So think about this ultimate roller coaster.

1. *Consider your ideal audience. Will it be a gentler ride for younger kids, or will it be a terrifying ride for adventure seekers? How do you want people to feel? Do you want people to feel scared? Nervous? Excited? Calm? Maybe a mix of all of those emotions?*

2. *What kind of theme will it have? See, every roller coaster has a theme. It might be a mountain theme or a space theme or pop culture theme. So create a theme for your roller coaster.*

3. *Decide on the features of your ride. Will it have a huge drop? A loop? A corkscrew turn?*

4. *Think of the physics and mechanics of your ride. How will you keep your coaster going from start to finish without stopping?*

For your model, you're going to use:

- *Duct tape*

- *Paper*

- *Cardboard*

- *A marble*

- *Plastic straws*

- *Popsicle sticks*

Don't forget to experiment and make tons of glorious mistakes. Ultimately, your design is going to be awesome, because it's yours and it's coming from your creative mind.

Feel overwhelmed?

Don't worry. You're going to go through the entire design process with your LAUNCH team. By the time you're finished, your roller coaster is going to be awesome!

INVESTIGATE THE CHALLENGE

After watching the video, jot down some observations. This could be anything you notice about this project. It could be ideas of what you'd want to create, details that stuck out to you, etc.

Observations	Questions

MEET WITH YOUR LAUNCH TEAMS

LISTEN TO YOUR AUDIENCE

You are going to build the ultimate roller coaster, which means you need to create the kind of ride that your classmates would actually enjoy. So try and keep that in mind as much as possible when you start planning things out.

CREATE A SURVEY

You want to make sure you know what your audience wants, right? So how do you figure this out? How do you go beyond assumptions to figure out their thoughts on roller coasters?

One of the options is a survey. Working as a team, you will create a survey for your classmates.

Think about the types of questions you want to ask. What do you need to know about your audience before you create a roller coaster for them?

Step One: Generate Questions

As a group, create a list of questions you would like to ask your audience. Feel free to use the sentence stems on the right if you are struggling with what to ask. Each member should have each question listed in his or her interactive notebook.

Survey Questions	Sentence Stems
1. 2. 3. 4.	• What is your favorite/least favorite _____? • When was the last time _____? • How do you feel about _____? • How often do you _____? • Why would _____? • Have you ever _____?

Step Two: Divide Up Your Questions

Next, divide up the questions so that each student gets one question. This will be your individual question.

My question is: _____

_____

_____

Step Three: Make It a Multiple-Choice Question

Individually, turn your survey questions into a multiple-choice survey question. Your survey question should at least have five options. Please use the table below:

Survey Question:
Option 1:
Option 2:
Option 3:
Option 4:
Option 5:

Step Four

Create a bar graph or a circle graph showing your results. Draw it out below:

Step Five

Share your results with your LAUNCH team. What trends do you notice? What will that mean in terms of creating the ultimate roller coaster?

LEARN MORE ABOUT YOUR ITEMS

Take some time to explore your items. You don't need to write anything here. Just play around with them. What are some of the possibilities that you see? What are some things that might come in handy? What are some design ideas that you might want to test out as you build a roller coaster?

Note: This is optional space where you can add any observations, notes, or ideas of how you might want to use these items in a roller coaster. You might draw a picture, make a web, or make a list.

PHASE TWO:
ASK A TON OF QUESTIONS

ASK QUESTIONS

Individual: Now that you have a clear picture of both the design challenge and your audience, you're going to create a set of questions you need to ask before planning out your roller coaster.

Think about it this way:
What kinds of questions do you have about the way roller coasters work? List your questions below:

1.

2.

3.

4.

5.

MEET WITH YOUR LAUNCH TEAMS

As a team, go round-robin and share your questions. As you add your questions to chart paper, individually add any additional questions that your group came up with below:

Phase Three:

Understand the Problem or Process

Meet with Your Launch Teams

Take your questions and begin researching online how roller coasters work. You might be curious what makes the tracks work or how they can continue to move from start to finish or how they go through a loop. Make sure to write your question, summarize your answer, and cite your source.

Question	Answer	Source

LAUNCH Notebook

Question	Answer	Source

Sketch Out Your Roller Coaster Ideas

Individual:

Sketch out some ideas for your roller coaster.

Phase Four:
Navigate the Ideas

CREATE A WEB

Individual:

Create a web showing all the things that a great roller coaster should have.

LAUNCH TEAM: BRAINSTORM

Share your ideas in one larger brainstorm. This could be a list or a web on chart paper. Make sure each group member gets a chance to add ideas. Draw your roller coaster concept below.

PHASE FIVE:
Create a Prototype

Meet with Your LAUNCH Teams

Create it! Use your supplies to see if you can make it. Write any notes of observations you see.

Phase Six:

Highlight What's Working and Fix What's Failing

Meet with Your Launch Teams

Spend some time testing out your roller coaster.

Jot down what's working and not working:

Stages	What's Working	What Needs to Be Improved
Example: Stage 1	The marble is moving fast.	The marble isn't going through the loop.

PHASE SEVEN:

LAUNCH IT!

Meet with Your Launch Teams

Launch It!

Now that you have finished with the roller coaster, you will launch the ride to your classmates.

- Option 1: Create a list of instructions showing how the roller coaster works.

- Option 2: Create a list of instructions with pictures showing how the roller coaster works.

- Option 3: Create a video showing how the roller coaster works.

- Option 4: Create an advertisement for the roller coaster.

- Option 5: Create a step-by-step storyboard showing what it would be like to ride your roller coaster.

Celebrate What You Learned!

Individual: Self-Reflection Questions

1. What did you learn from this experience? Would you want to do this again?

2. How well did you work with your group?

3. What were some creative risks that you took?

4. Which phase in the LAUNCH Cycle was the best for you and why?

MORE FROM DAVE BURGESS Consulting, Inc.

Teach Like a PIRATE

Increase Student Engagement, Boost Your Creativity, and Transform Your Life as an Educator
By Dave Burgess (@BurgessDave)

Teach Like a PIRATE is the *New York Times'* best-selling book that has sparked a worldwide educational revolution. It is part inspirational manifesto that ignites passion for the profession and part practical road map, filled with dynamic strategies to dramatically increase student engagement. Translated into multiple languages, its message resonates with educators who want to design outrageously creative lessons and transform school into a life-changing experience for students.

P is for PIRATE

Inspirational ABC's for Educators

By Dave and Shelley Burgess (@Burgess_Shelley)

Teaching is an adventure that stretches the imagination and calls for creativity every day! In *P is for Pirate*, husband and wife team, Dave and Shelley Burgess, encourage and inspire educators to make their classrooms fun and exciting places to learn. Tapping into years of personal experience and drawing on the insights of more than seventy educators, the authors offer a wealth of ideas for making learning and teaching more fulfilling than ever before.

The Innovator's Mindset

Empower Learning, Unleash Talent, and Lead a Culture of Creativity

By George Couros (@gcouros)

The traditional system of education requires students to hold their questions and compliantly stick to the scheduled curriculum. But our job as educators is to provide new and better opportunities for our students. It's time to recognize that compliance doesn't foster innovation, encourage critical thinking, or inspire creativity—and those are the skills our students need to succeed. In *The Innovator's Mindset*, George Couros encourages teachers and administrators to empower their learners to wonder, to explore—and to become forward-thinking leaders.

Pure Genius

Building a Culture of Innovation and Taking 20% Time to the Next Level

By Don Wettrick (@DonWettrick)

For far too long, schools have been bastions of boredom, killers of creativity, and way too comfortable with compliance and conformity. In *Pure Genius*, Don Wettrick explains how collaboration—with experts, students, and other educators—can help you create interesting, and even life-changing, opportunities for learning. Wettrick's book inspires and equips educators with a systematic blueprint for teaching innovation in any school.

Learn Like a PIRATE

Empower Your Students to Collaborate, Lead, and Succeed

By Paul Solarz (@PaulSolarz)

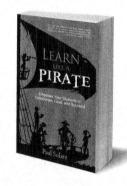

Today's job market demands that students be prepared to take responsibility for their lives and careers. We do them a disservice if we teach them how to earn passing grades without equipping them to take charge of their education. In *Learn Like a Pirate*, Paul Solarz explains how to design classroom experiences that encourage students to take risks and explore their passions in a stimulating, motivating, and supportive environment where improvement, rather than grades, is the focus. Discover how student-led classrooms help students thrive and develop into self-directed, confident citizens who are capable of making smart, responsible decisions, all on their own.

Ditch That Textbook

Free Your Teaching and Revolutionize
Your Classroom

By Matt Miller (@jmattmiller)

Textbooks are symbols of centuries-old education. They're often outdated as soon as they hit students' desks. Acting "by the textbook" implies compliance and a lack of creativity. It's time to ditch those textbooks—and those textbook assumptions about learning! In *Ditch That Textbook*, teacher and blogger Matt Miller encourages educators to throw out meaningless, pedestrian teaching and learning practices. He empowers them to evolve and improve on old, standard teaching methods. *Ditch That Textbook* is a support system, toolbox, and manifesto to help educators free their teaching and revolutionize their classrooms.

50 Things You Can Do with Google Classroom

By Alice Keeler and Libbi Miller
(@AliceKeeler, @MillerLibbi)

It can be challenging to add new technology to the classroom, but it's a must if students are going to be well-equipped for the future. Alice Keeler and Libbi Miller shorten the learning curve by providing a thorough overview of the Google Classroom App. Part of Google Apps for Education (GAfE), Google Classroom was specifically designed to help teachers save time by streamlining the process of going digital. Complete with screenshots, *50 Things You Can Do with Google Classroom* provides ideas and step-by-step instructions to help teachers implement this powerful tool.

140 Twitter Tips for Educators

Get Connected, Grow Your Professional
Learning Network, and Reinvigorate Your Career

By Brad Currie, Billy Krakower, and Scott Rocco
(@bradmcurrie, @wkrakower, @ScottRRocco)

Whatever questions you have about education or about how you can be even better at your job, you'll find ideas, resources, and a vibrant network of professionals ready to help you on Twitter. In *140 Twitter Tips for Educators*, #Satchat hosts and founders of Evolving Educators, Brad Currie, Billy Krakower, and Scott Rocco offer step-by-step instructions to help you master the basics of Twitter, build an online following, and become a Twitter rock star.

Master the Media

*How Teaching Media Literacy Can
Save Our Plugged-in World*

By Julie Smith (@julnilsmith)

Written to help teachers and parents educate the next generation, *Master the Media* explains the history, purpose, and messages behind the media. The point isn't to get kids to unplug; it's to help them make informed choices, understand the difference between truth and lies, and discern perception from reality. Critical thinking leads to smarter decisions—and it's why media literacy can save the world.

The Zen Teacher

*Creating FOCUS, SIMPLICITY, and TRANQUILITY in
the Classroom*

By Dan Tricarico (@TheZenTeacher)

Teachers have incredible power to influence, even improve, the future. In *The Zen Teacher*, educator, blogger, and speaker Dan Tricarico provides practical, easy-to-use techniques to help teachers be their best—unrushed and fully focused—so they can maximize their performance and improve their quality of life. In this introductory guide, Dan Tricarico explains what it means to develop a Zen practice—something that has nothing to do with religion and everything to do with your ability to thrive in the classroom.

eXPlore Like a Pirate

*Gamification and Game-Inspired Course Design
to Engage, Enrich, and Elevate Your Learners*

By Michael Matera (@MrMatera)

Are you ready to transform your classroom into an experiential world that flourishes on collaboration and creativity? Then set sail with classroom game designer and educator, Michael Matera, as he reveals the possibilities and power of game-based learning. In *eXPlore Like a Pirate*, Matera serves as your experienced guide to help you apply the most motivational techniques of gameplay to your classroom. You'll learn gamification strategies that will work with and enhance (rather than replace) your current curriculum and discover how these engaging methods can be applied to any grade level or subject.

Your School Rocks...So Tell People!

Passionately Pitch and Promote the Positives Happening on Your Campus

By Ryan McLane and Eric Lowe
(@McLane_Ryan, @EricLowe21)

Great things are happening in your school every day. The problem is, no one beyond your school walls knows about them. School principals Ryan McLane and Eric Lowe want to help you get the word out! In *Your School Rocks...So Tell People!*, McLane and Lowe offer more than seventy immediately actionable tips along with easy-to-follow instructions and links to video tutorials. This practical guide will equip you to create an effective and manageable communication strategy using social media tools. Learn how to keep your students' families and community connected, informed, and excited about what's going on in your school.

The Classroom Chef

Sharpen your lessons. Season your classes. Make math meaningful.

By John Stevens and Matt Vaudrey
(@stevens009, @MrVaudrey)

In *The Classroom Chef*, math teachers and instructional coaches John Stevens and Matt Vaudrey share their secret recipes, ingredients, and tips for serving up lessons that engage students and help them "get" math. You can use these ideas and methods as-is, or better yet, tweak them and create your own enticing educational meals. The message the authors share is that, with imagination and preparation, every teacher can be a Classroom Chef.

How Much Water Do We Have?

5 Success Principles for Conquering Any Change and Thriving in Times of Change

by Pete Nunweiler with Kris Nunweiler

In *How Much Water Do We Have?* Pete Nunweiler identifies five key elements—information, planning, motivation, support, and leadership—that are necessary for the success of any goal, life transition, or challenge. Referring to these elements as the 5 Waters of Success, Pete explains that like the water we drink, you need them to thrive in today's rapidly paced world. If you're feeling stressed out, overwhelmed, or uncertain at work or at home, pause and look for the signs of dehydration. Learn how to find, acquire, and use the 5 Waters of Success—so you can share them with your team and family members.

Bring John Spencer
to Your School or Event

John Spencer is passionate about seeing educators embrace design thinking and creativity. Over the past few years, he has shared this vision for creative classrooms with a variety of audiences, including his speech in the White House about the future of education and his TEDx Talk on creativity. John offers an engaging, thought-provoking, and humorous style through his keynotes, full-day workshops, and online professional development. He offers the unique perspective of being a published author, the co-founder of a successful startup, an award-winning classroom teacher, and a college professor. He uses this blend of classroom experience, industry experience, and research experience to craft innovative, holistic, and practical learning experiences in a style that is approachable and relevant.

WHAT PEOPLE ARE SAYING ABOUT JOHN SPENCER

"John's classroom and research expertise on project-based learning, design thinking, and blended literacy allows him to offer realistic and practical suggestions to move teachers forward. John's amazing creativity can be seen in his humor, writing, drawings, and engaging presentation style. If you are looking for someone to go beyond the '50 Apps in 50 Minutes' style of professional development to a practical, student-centered pedagogy, then John Spencer is whom you should call."

"John Spencer is a fantastic speaker. He will inspire you and push your thinking to new heights. His mixture of content, storytelling, and humor makes for a great keynote."

"John inspires and empowers. I rarely say that something transforms my practice, but this design thinking workshop changed the way I teach."

POPULAR MESSAGES FROM JOHN SPENCER

John often speaks on creativity, design thinking, research-based student engagement, and meaningful technology integration. Most of his workshops and keynotes are tailored specifically for your audience and include a set of resources customized for the audience. Here are a few of his most recent examples:

- The Creative Classroom: Boosting Creativity and Innovation Through Design Thinking

- We Want Kids to Be Creative but How Do We Assess That?

- The Seven Types of Creative Teachers

- This Is The Future of Education

- In the Zone: Maximizing Student Engagement with Flow Theory

- Epic Engagement: Lesson Planning Through the Lens of Story

- Five Authentic Assessment Strategies You Can Use Tomorrow

- The Seven Stages in the Technology Journey

- It Is Personal: A New Vision for Personalized Learning

CONNECT

Connect with John Spencer for more information about bringing him to your event.

- E-mail: john@educationrethink.com

- Twitter: @spencerideas

- Blog: spencerideas.org

- YouTube: sketchyvideos.com

BRING A.J. JULIANI
TO YOUR SCHOOL OR EVENT

A.J. Juliani brings a high-energy, fun, and engaging style of presentation through keynotes, full-day workshops, and online professional development offerings. His mix of personal stories from the classroom, real-world examples, and research-based insights lead to a learning opportunity for everyone in attendance. A.J. has worked at all levels of the K-12 spectrum and has the lens of a parent as well. He will encourage educators to not only be intentional about innovation, but also focus on how our practice needs to always be centered on the student experience.

What People are Saying About A.J. Juliani

"I was captivated by your presentation. Honestly, most keynote addresses usually don't hit home, but yours definitely got my brain working overtime."

"The best keynote I've been to in a long time. Thank you for sharing with us. I hope to be mindful of this inspirational feeling always."

"I really can't explain how awesome A.J. Juliani is! Inspiring, funny and, more importantly, making me reflect on my practice."

Popular Messages from A.J. Juliani

Many of A.J.'s presentations are created specifically for your event, audience, and school. To get a sense of the topics A.J. presents on most, here are some previous keynote presentations he has done in the past:

- The Power of Inquiry and Choice: 20% Time and Genius Hour Projects

- Intentional Innovation: How to Guide Risk-Taking, Build Creative Capacity, and Lead Change

- Student-Centered Classrooms for Today's Student: Engaging All Learners Through Choice, Technology, and Innovative Practices

- Technology With a Purpose: Empowering Students With Choice and Technology

- Design Thinking and the Maker Movement in K-12

CONNECT

Connect with A.J. Juliani for more information about bringing him to your event.

- E-mail: ajjuliani@gmail.com

- Twitter: @ajjuliani

- Blog: ajjuliani.com

ABOUT THE AUTHORS

John Spencer is passionate about empowering students to become creative thinkers through design thinking. After spending twelve years as an urban middle school teacher, John is now a full-time professor of Educational Technology and a leader in creativity, design thinking, and student engagement. John has a goal of making something new each day. He is the co-founder of two educational startups and the co-author of a top-selling children's book.

As a dad, he loves to make stuff with his children, whether it's writing comics like "Taco Tony," building a model roller coaster with recycled material, or making a city with LEGO bricks (which are awesome until you step on them at four in the morning).

John shares his vision for creative classrooms through his blog (spencerideas.org) and his illustrated videos (sketchyvideos.com). You can connect with him on Twitter (@spencerideas) or on his Facebook page (https://www.facebook.com/EdRethink).

A.J. Juliani is a leading educator in the area of innovation, design thinking, and inquiry-based learning. Juliani has worked as a Middle and High School English Teacher, a K-12 Technology Staff Developer, and is currently an administrator for a public school district with the title of Education and Technology Innovation Specialist.

A.J. is the author of *Inquiry and Innovation in the Classroom* and *Learning By Choice*, books centered on student agency, choice, innovative learning, and engagement. As a parent of four young children, A.J. believes we must be intentional about innovation in order to create a better future of learning for all of our students. You can connect with A.J. on his blog, "Intentional Innovation" (located at ajjuliani.com), or through Twitter (@ajjuliani).

TheLaunchCycle.com
#LAUNCHBOOK

CPSIA information can be obtained
at www.ICGtesting.com
Printed in the USA
LVOW13s0524300717

543085LV00001B/7/P